PRINCIPLES OF ISLAMIC JURISPRUDENCE

Muḥammad al-Bāqir al-Ṣadr

PRINCIPLES OF ISLAMIC JURISPRUDENCE

According to Shiʿi Law

Translated by Arif Abdul Hussain
Edited by Hamid Algar and Saʿeed Bahmanpour

ICAS Press

British Library Cataloguing-in-Publication Data
A catalogue record for this book is available from the
British Library

ISBN 1 904063 12 8

This edition first published 2003

Published by
Islamic College for Advanced Studies Press (ICAS)
133 High Road, Willesden, London NW10 2SW

Contents

First Editor's Note

The principles of jurisprudence (*uṣūl al-fiqh*) may be described in essence as the legal philosophy of Islam, a science embracing both reflection on the purposes of the sacred law (*Sharīʿā*) and the methods of deriving specific rulings from the sources of the law. Given that law is the primary means by which Islam is translated into reality in both individual and social life, study of the principles of jurisprudence has always held a central position in Islamic scholarship.

The present work is the translation of *Durūs fī ʿilm al-fiqh*, a series of lectures on the discipline given by a contemporary master of the Islamic sciences, al-Shahid Muhammad Bāqir al-Ṣadr (d. 1980). His intellectual achievements were manifold, and the numerous books that he wrote on philosophy, theology and contemporary issues represent a major contribution to contemporary Islamic thought. Like all his writings, the present book is marked by clarity of style and argumentation, features particularly helpful when dealing with a potentially abstruse subject such as the principles of jurisprudence. Prefaced to the complete translation of the lectures is an extract from another work of al-Ṣadr, *al-Maʿālim al-jadīda li'l-uṣūl*, which presents in summary form a history of the discipline, particularly as cultivated by the scholars of Shi'a Islam. A glossary of technical terms complements the text.

H. Algar

Second Editor's Note

The book you are about to read is a translation of one of the most famous academic works of the late Ayatullah Sayyid Muḥammad Bāqir al-Ṣadr (1934–1980), written in plain language to introduce the beginners into the science of 'the principles of jurisprudence'. It is the first book of a series organized in three different levels in terms of depth and comprehensiveness to help the student to understand the subject in a gradual and graded manner. Originally given the title *Durūs fī 'ilm al-uṣūl* (Discourses in Jurisprudence), but normally known as *Ḥalaqāt al-uṣūl* (Courses in Jurisprudence), the book was a revolutionary attempt intended to renovate the teaching material and the curriculum of Shī'a seminaries throughout the world. Indeed in many teaching centers it replaced the book *al-Ma'ālim* written by Shaykh Ḥasan b. Shahīd al-Thānī which had been taught to students of jurisprudence since the twelfth century AH.

Ayatullah Sadr, who was renowned for his genius, was highly concerned about the methods and the materials of education in religious seminaries and set out to refresh and renovate both those methods and materials. The structure of his books – including the present book – is well organized and logically constructed, moving step by step, building each stage on what has been established previously.

It is for all these reasons that this book was chosen for translation by the Islamic College for Advanced Studies as a guide to the beginners and as an introduction to the science of Islamic jurisprudence according to the Shī'a school of law in English Language.

The translator, Shaykh Arif Abd al-Hussain, is an expert in the field himself and has been a student and a teacher of Islamic law and jurisprudence since 1985. He has deep insights into the subject and has dedicated several years of his academic career teaching Islamic jurisprudence and other related subjects in Al-Mahdi Institute of Birmingham, where he has been the director for several years.

I hope the book would benefit the students of Islamic jurisprudence and would enhance Western understanding of this subtle and delicate subject.

Mohammad Saeed Bahmanpour
London, July 2003

A Short Biography of Martyr Ayatullah al-Ṣadr

Martyr al-Ṣadr was born in the Iraqi city of Kadhimiyya on 25 Dhil Qaʿda 1353 HL (1934–35 CE).

After completing his primary education in Kadhimiyya, he moved to Najaf, a very important centre of learning in Islam's history. Like other Muslim scholars of his time, he managed to reach an advanced stage in Islamic studies before he had even completed his primary secular education. At Najaf he enrolled for advanced Islamic studies at the age of 12 and attended what is known as *khārij* (graduate studies), where students are instructed in various branches of Islamic thought and legal matters. When he was 15 he gave up *taqlīd* (lit. emulation – the following by a layman of a learned scholar 'jurist' in matters of religious practice) since he had reached the age of taklīf (i.e. the age of 15 when it becomes incumbent on a male Muslim to uphold the precepts of religion).

Having attained the degree of *ijtihād* at the tender age of 17, he continued his studies at the university in Najaf under the supervision of its renowned academics, graduating in 1378/1958–59 CE) to become an authoritative *mujtahid* (independent legal pragmatist). His teachers acclaimed him for his academic brilliance.

He started doing in earnest what he had always loved to do: writing, researching and lecturing. His first work, which discussed his own pioneering approach to *uṣūl al-fiqh* (principles of jurisprudence), was entitled *Purpose of Thought in the Principles of Jurisprudence.* A second scientific work, in which al-Ṣadr looked into the events of Islamic history that immediately followed the death of the Messenger of Allah(s), was published under the title *Fadak in History*. He later started planning to publish a number of studies outlining Islamic thought as a faith and socio-political system in a modern scientific style compatible with the prevailing requirements. In these studies, he would bring Islam to the fore as an ideology, order and system, in a picture that would appeal to the contemporary world. Sayyid al-Ṣadr also showed the failure of temporal schools as well as of materialistic ideologies and theories that disengage humans from their relationship with divine revelation. He then began work on his great *Our Philosophy* in which he presented Islamic philosophical thinking in an new manner. In *Our Economics*, which followed, he investigated and scrutinized modern economic schools of thought and compared what contemporary materialistic culture, both capitalist and socialist, has offered as (doctrinal) solutions for the tragedy of modern economic life with the solution offered by the Islamic economic system. In this study, he highlighted major drawbacks and weaknesses inherent in all materialistic economic systems and showed the superiority of Islam's economic doctrine over its rivals in all its aspects, i.e. in basis, principles, precepts and details.

He had planned for the second work in his ideological trilogy on Islam to be a study entitled *Our Society*, but in response to demand and the requests of many readers, he published *Our Economics* in its place. Sadly, circumstances militated against the publishing of *Our Society* as the third work in the trilogy. The intelligentsia waited in great expectation and longing for this sequel to be published, but Sayyid al-Ṣadr was unable to bring the work to light before he was assassinated.

The new Islamic thinking elucidated by the genius of the Imām as-Ṣadr, whether at the level of the new Islamic culture or at the level of classical studies, has created a strong ideological wave that gradually swept over the intellectual landscape in various Islamic countries, especially Iraq and Iran. This new Islamic thinking greatly helped to safeguard the Muslim cultural mind against foreign ideological invasions and to prepare the ground for organized political action aimed at attaining an Islamic society based on an Islamic system and tenets of the Holy Qur'ān.

The Islamic movement developed from a state of passivity along the ideological lines set out by Sayyid as-Ṣadr. The movement was making huge efforts to stop the foreign ideological onslaught and cure the cultural and ideological ailments that became epidemic among Muslim intellectuals as a result of the infiltration of foreign culture into the very fabric of our scientific institutions and cultural organizations. In the new stage Islamic ideology came to the fore, armed with the theories of Imām as-Ṣadr, who, having barred the road to the invading ideology's attempt to dominate over Islamic institutions and culture, as well as the minds of men, had then chased it right inside its fortifications.

Martyr Sayyid al-Ṣadr took a unique role in revolutionizing the Islamic situation in Iraq, educating its activists and directing them both intellectually and politically. He played a pivotal role in educating the Islamic cultural elite and elements of the Islamic movement and establishing an activist Islamic organization, whose development and direction he guided. He also played a leading role in activating and energizing the Islamic seminaries, ideologically and politically. Strongholds of the new ideological and political activity existed throughout Iraq, in particular in the seminaries of Najaf Holy City. Among these were the League of *'Ulama* (scholars), the Literary League, the Islamic Sciences School, the Publishing Forum, Imām al Jawād Schools, the Administrative Corps of the Supreme Religious Authority and the late Imām Sayyid al-Hakim's cultural, social and political projects: all took inspiration, direction and guidance from as-Ṣadr, thanks to his intellectual prowess.

After the death of the late brave yet patient Imām al-Ḥakīm, Sayyid al-Ṣadr assumed leadership of the Muslim masses in Iraq. He started organizing the religious authority apparatus, establishing a religious relations network that connects the popular base with the religious authority through the clergy and the culturally qualified cadres in the towns and cities. Before assuming the mantle of Supreme Religious Leader, he had prepared a comprehensive, well-researched and inspiring treatise on 'the properly guided religious authority', which was the first theoretical work in the history of the Shi'i religious authority to attempt to reorganize its apparatus, as well as to make it efficient and forward-looking.

The enormous and widespread following of his supreme religious authority (*marja'iyya*) in Shi'i quarters coincided with the triumph of the Islamic revolution in Iran. He was the first to support it with vigour. Notwithstanding his distinguished position, he considered himself duty-bound, from a religious perspective, to toe the line of Imām Khomeini and to protect the Islamic revolution and support it zealously. This stance he bequeathed to his students and followers. He reiterated this clearly in his well-known letter to his students in Iran during the early days of the victory of the Islamic revolution, which was led by Imām Khomeini. In that letter, he said, 'The duty of each one of you and of every individual whose good fortune leads him to be part of this pioneering Islamic experience is to spare no effort or means in the service of this experience;

nor should he spare any effort while construction for the sake of Islam is underway. No limit should be imposed on efforts while the force of Islam hoists high the banner of the cause. This new constructive project is in need of the efforts of all individuals, no matter how small. It should also be clear that all should embrace, pay allegiance to and protect the interests of Sayyid Khomeini's religious authority, which has embodied Islam's hopes in today's Iran, and should desire to become assimilated into its great existence for the sake of its great goal. The good religious authority is not a person, but a goal and a path to it. Any religious authority that attains that goal is a good one, in which case it should be served with all devotion. Religious authority in Iran should abstain from and reject everything that may weaken or does not contribute to safeguarding it.

After victory of the Islamic revolution, Sayyid al-Ṣadr started to intensify the activities of his Islamic revolutionary movement in Iraq. Using cassette tapes, lectures and letters sent to his students and representatives both inside and outside Iraq, he called upon the Iraqi people to wage an overall Islamic revolution against the Baʿthist domination of power in Iraq. He constantly emphasized the need to revolt in the face of tyrants and to work towards the application of Islamic teachings in all Islamic countries, rather in every corner of the earth. He reiterated that it may be necessary to sacrifice one's own life for the triumph of the true religion of Islam and for the defence of the victimized and the oppressed. He was well known for his last three appeals to the Iraqi people. Here are some passages of these appeals. In his first appeal dated 20 Rajab 1399 HL (1978 CE), he wrote, 'O People of my forefathers! I assure you that I am with you fully, nor shall I abandon you in your ordeal. I shall sacrifice the last drop of my blood. I confirm to those at the helm that the oppression directed against the Iraqi people, through the force of iron and fire, which deprived them of the simplest rights and freedoms to observe their religious rites, cannot continue. Nor can it always be handled by force and repression. If force were a permanent and decisive remedy, the pharaohs and tyrants would have survived. They stopped broadcasting the 'call for prayer' and we remained patient; they stopped broadcasting Friday prayers, yet we remained patient; they imposed restrictions on staging commemorative ceremonies for the martyrdom of Imām Hussain, nevertheless, we showed forbearance; they imposed a siege on mosques and inundated them with their spies, yet we persevered; they launched campaigns aimed at coercing people to join the ranks of their party, yet we remained patient; they said, 'It is only a transitional period during which people must be galvanized', nevertheless, we showed resilience. But until when? How long is this transitional period to continue? Is a period of ten years of absolute rule not enough to prepare an appropriate atmosphere for the Iraqi people to choose their own way? And if a period of ten years of absolute rule has not allowed you, O you who are in power, to convince people to join your party other than by coercion, what do you hope for?

He then added, 'In the name of human dignity, I demand the release of those who were arbitrarily arrested and the cessation of summary detention that takes place outside the domain of the judiciary. Lastly, I demand, in the name of all of you and in the name of the values you uphold, to allow the people the opportunity truly to exercise their right in running the affairs of the country by holding elections in which a council representing the *umma* (community) could truly emerge.

'I know that these demands will cost me dearly, perhaps even my life, but these are not demands that could die out with a person's death. They are the yearnings of an *umma*, the will of an *umma*, in whose psyche roams the spirit of Muḥammad, ʿAlī and the chosen descendants of Muḥammad and his companions, and that will never die.'

In his second appeal to the Iraqi people, on 10 Shaʿban 1399 HL (1979 CE), he continued, 'O my dear Iraqi people! O Muslim masses of Iraq, who have stood up to protect your religion, dignity, freedom and might and for all the values and ideals you believe in. O Great *umma*! Today you are experiencing hard times at the hands of assassins and butchers, who are astounded by the wrath of the awakening masses, after they have chained them in irons and instilled fear and terror in their hearts. The bloodletting villains imagine that they have robbed the masses of their esteem and dignity, stripped them of their great faith, the religion of Muḥammad, so as to turn these brave, believing millions of proud Iraqi people into toys and tools to manipulate as they wish, into which they feed forcibly allegiance to Aflaq [the founder and theorist of the Baʿth party] and his like – agents of missionaries and imperialism – in place of allegiance to Muḥammad and ʿAlī. Yet the masses are always stronger than tyrants, no matter how harsh their tyranny becomes. Thus, the tyrants were surprised to discover that the *umma* still pulsates with life and retains the ability to speak its mind. Consequently, the tyrants lashed out at tens of thousands of believers and honest sons of this dignified country, meting out imprisonment, arrests, torture and death sentences; in the forefront of these victims were the *Mujāhidīn* elite of the *ʿulama* [religious scholars], who report the death from torture of one after another.'

He went on, 'and I announce to you, O my sons, that I am determined to tread the path of martyrdom. This, therefore, may be the last that you will hear from me, as the gates of heaven open to receive the convoys of martyrs. Allah shall ordain victory for you. How sweet is martyrdom in whose praise the Messenger of Allah said, 'It is a good deed in which no misdeed could prevail, for in martyrdom, the martyr shall have all his sins, no matter how gross, forgiven.' It is the duty of every Muslim in Iraq and every Iraqi outside Iraq to do all that is in his capacity – even if it cost him his life – to maintain *jihād* and struggle in order to lift this burden off the chest of Iraq, to liberate it from the hands of the inhuman criminals and to establish an honest, unique and good rule of government that is based on Islam. May Allah's peace and blessings be with you.'

In his last appeal, the date of which is unknown, he said, 'O my dear people of Iraq! O you great *umma*, in this difficult and turbulent moment and at this juncture of your *jihād*, I would like to address all groups and sects, Arabs and Kurds alike, Sunni and Shi'a alike, because the calamity that has been inflected upon us knows no sectarian or ethnic divide; the calamity is universal. Therefore, a fighting stance, heroic retaliation and cohesion should be the living reality of all the Iraqi people. From a position of responsibility in this *umma*, I have spared no effort to sacrifice my well-being for the sake of the Shi'a and the Sunni in equal measure, as well as for the sake of Arab and Kurd equally. This stems from my belief in defending the message that unites them all and the faith that unites them all. I have lived my existence for nothing other than Islam, which is the road to salvation and the goal of all. I am with you, O my Sunni brother and son, just as much I am with you, O my Shi'a brother and son! I am with you both in the same measure you are with Islam, and in just as much as you bear this great flame to salvage Iraq and rid it of the nightmare of oppression, subservience and persecution. The despotic regime [*tāghūt*] and its followers try to suggest to our noble Sunni sons that it is a matter of Shi'a and Sunni, so as to separate Sunni from their real struggle against the common enemy. I want to say to you, O sons of 'Alī and Ḥussain and sons of Abu Bakr and 'Umar! The fight is not between Shi'a and Sunni rule. 'Alī unsheathed his sword in defence of the Sunni rule represented by the Guided Caliphs, which was based on Islam and justice, as he fought during the wars waged against the apostates [in the aftermath of the death of the Prophet] under the standard of the first Caliph Abu Bakr. All of us should fight for the banner of Islam to be hoisted high and to march under that banner, no matter what colour its proponent. The Sunni rule that bore the flag of Islam elicited the *fatawa* of the Shi'a clergy, half a century ago, of the necessity to wage *jihād* for it. Hundreds of thousands of Shi'a marched out and sacrificed their lives unselfishly to safeguard the standard of Islam and in order to protect the Sunni rule that was based on Islam. This present de facto rule is not Sunni rule, even though the dominant group is historically related to Sunnism.'

Rumours in Iraq abound that Martyr al-Ṣadr was planning to leave Iraq. Delegations to show support, solidarity and allegiance started converging on his residence in the Holy City of Najaf, calling on him to remain in Iraq. This was tantamount to a popular mobilization to prepare the Iṛaqi people for its confrontation with the regime on the one hand and to demonstrate the influence the Martyr could exert on the populace before the very eyes of the regime on the other hand; however, Sayyid al-Ṣadr saw fit to stop the march of the delegations so as to prepare other steps for a revolutionary movement for which he was equipping the *umma*.

The Baʿthist authorities arrested Sayyid al-Ṣadr on 17 Rajab 1399 HL (1978 CE). His arrest triggered a big popular uprising in the Holy City of Najaf, led by his sister, Bintulhudā, which culminated in armed confrontation between the masses and the regime's security forces. This uprising was accompanied by other popular protests in major Iraqi cities, such as Basra, Diyala, Kadhimiyya and others, which brought pressure to bear on the regime to release Sayyid as-Ṣadr temporarily.

On witnessing this popular rallying of support of martyr Imām al-Ṣadr, which prevented it from eradicating him, the Baʿthist regime resorted to a new plan in its confrontation with the Martyr Imām . It laid siege to the house where he used to live, virtually placing him under house arrest, and preventing the faithful and the *'ulama* from making contact with him. The regime succeeded in its plan. This situation continued right up to the time when he was last arrested on 19 Jamādi al-ʿUla 1400 HL (1979-80 CE), followed by the arrest of his sister, Bintulhuda. The malicious Baʿthist authorities murdered the Imām soon after his arrest. He returned to his Lord as a mujāhid and martyr, with forbearance and anticipating the good rewards of Allah, may He be pleased with him.

Shahīd Bāqir al-Ṣadr and the Islamic Renaissance

Shahid Bāqir's intellectual maturity occurred at the most critical time of contemporary Islamic history. It was a period when Islam faced ideological and socio-political challenges. On the one hand, dialectical materialist ideologies had begun to win recruits among the youth and intelligentsia in the university campuses. On the other hand, political organizations that openly advocated foreign domination of Islamic countries were fast becoming a formidable force by recruiting armies of volunteers and highly qualified personnel to conspire against the Muslim nation. Thus, citizens of the Muslim states started to feel like outsiders in their own lands. The renaissance project of Martyr Ayatullah al-Ṣadr focused on three aspects of change:

1. Ideological Change

He realized that the Islamic ideology had become the victim of a very powerful alien influence. Therefore a new methodological approach was needed, a total re-thinking of the Islamic ideology in light of the new developments. The ultimate goal was to come up with a method that would restore confidence among Muslim academicians in the relevance and effectiveness of the new Ideology. To achieve this goal he set about establishing the following foundations of change.

a) The reinterpretation of the canonical texts in light of new developments.

b) Renewing research and curricula in theology schools (*ḥawza 'ilmiyya*) and institutions for Islamic studies. He called for the introduction of contemporary methods of research and a new hermeneutics that would produce scholars qualified to participate in solving contemporary problems for society.

c) Portraying Islam as a comprehensive and harmonious system, which emanates from a deep-rooted philosophical vision for man and universe, augmented by philosophical proof and logical evidence. Here he rejected the method of both Muslim liberals and of radical traditionalism.

d) Deconstructing alien ideologies in a manner that would expose their inherent contradictions and inability to come up with sound solutions for the problems affecting humanity.

e) Preparing an active generation of intellectuals from within the ranks of religious scholars and university students, with a view to keeping such intellectuals abreast of Islamic culture and new Islamic thinking and pushing them to the forefront of ideological confrontation with adverse atheist and materialistic ideologies.

2. Social Change
Imām al-Ṣadr saw that social change and social justice in the *umma* (Islamic community) could be realized only through a trusted leadership fully qualified to champion social change and participate in the struggle for social justice. According to him, the theory of 'religious authority' (*marja'iyyah*) was the only apparatus available to deal with complex social situations. However, the passive attitude of some within this religious authority and their support for the status quo made this task almost impossible. Any effective and successful social change therefore needed to start with the creation by the religious establishment itself of a wide ideological base within society that encompasses conscious Islamic understanding, such as the understanding that reiterates that Islam is a comprehensive and complete system of life.

3. Political Change
For Ayatullah al-Ṣadr the process of overall transformation of the society could be achieved only through the application of the revealed laws of Allah in full and in all fields of human activity. This required the establishment of an Islamic state that would be responsible for applying the *Sharī'ā* in all aspects of life. Since an Islamic state is an ideological state, it was important to prepare the *ummah* ideologically. Ideological preparation could be achieved by disseminating Islamic political awareness among its members. An ignorant and apolitical people could easily be oppressed by the establishment and in order to safeguard human political freedom the *ummah* had to be properly educated in Islamic political theory and constitutionalism.

Outstanding Contributions of Martyr al-Ṣadr

Shahid al-Ṣadr stands out as one of the most prolific scholars of twentieth-century Islam. His contribution to Islamic political, legal, economic and philosophical thought is still evident from the many works and papers he published in these areas. His achievements may be summarized as follows.

1. His creativity in the techniques of methodical research in Islamic studies
The most significant characteristic of Imām al-Ṣadr's ideology is his logical methodology, such as is rarely found in his contemporaries. Sayyid al-Ṣadr possessed an organized methodical mind that did not deal with an idea without placing it in a coordinated logical mould. He could often be found discussing and criticizing an idea, yet imparting to it an evidential form and a uniform methodical style, with the result that he explained it even better than its original proponent. The main points of methodical innovation in the thinking of the Shahid al-Ṣadr could be summarized as follows:

a) a comprehensive uniform vision of the heritage of the revelation, which strives to present Islam as an overall system, whether in its faith fundamentals or its juridical structure.

b) discovery of a system of inductive subjective logic, which he expounded in his book *The Logical Principles of Induction*, and its employment in religious research, in addition to the evidential logical syllogism.

c) clarity of expression, beauty of composition, exactitude in performance and proportionality in literary and logical terms.

d) logical analysis of an idea into its components and composites and exposition of the interrelationships between them.

e) deconstruction of complex subjects and the giving to each constituent part its logical share of study; investigating the probabilities of research and giving due consideration to possible hypotheses at the level of scientific study and research.

f) arranging the points and subjects of research in a manner that places each of them in its appropriate logical sequence; studying the contradictory idea and challenging it logically and scientifically.

Although Islamic scholarship from the first century of *hijrah* to the contemporary era has always engaged in interdisciplinary studies and research, al-Ṣadr's *Our Philosophy* and *Our Economics* were groundbreaking projects in the Muslim world. What separates him from other generations of Muslim thinkers and theorists is the following methods of approach:

a) depth in contemplating opposing ideas and infinite exactness in studying and presenting ideas.

b) extensive and comprehensive research into the output of other schools of thought, whether in the area of lively dialogue or theoretical research or in the real world of practical application.

c) a solid, objective, logical style in studying opposing ideas, which keeps the subject researched separate from anything that may disturb logical contemplation, such as resorting to taunting and mockery, sharp criticism or the like.

d) documenting scientific research and largely depending upon accredited references in studying the alternative ideas.

e) superiority of logic, emanating from his superior scientific ability, which equipped him to challenge opposing ideas in a fight that did not leave it any escape route but to concede defeat and surrender.

2. Handling contemporary human problems and issues

The ideological achievements of Ayatullah al-Ṣadr are characterized by their serious tone and focus on the issues facing contemporary man and the proposition of modern Islamic solutions for them. Each one of these works, such as *Our Economics, Our Philosophy, Interest-free Banking in Islam, Islam Leads Life, The Manifest Edicts, Lessons in the Science of the Principles of Jurisprudence, The Logical Principles of Induction* and other major intellectual achievements, deal with either a general contemporary problem or a special problem experienced by a particular section of society. Such problems, as he recognized, have a bearing on the present and the future of the *umma*.

3. Scientific innovation in the field of Islamic studies

Martyr Ayatullah al-Ṣadr practised the critical editing of texts in higher studies at the University of Najaf for more than a quarter of a century. He contributed to the ideological output in some of the most important fields of Islamic knowledge, especially philosophy, jurisprudence (*fiqh*) and principles of jurisprudence. His scientific work in those fields stands out as comprehensive, thorough and innovative. He managed to decipher the inherited wisdom of learned men of the past and fathom the thoughts of his contemporaries. He developed what he found worthy of development and took issue with whatever he saw as point of contention. So immense was his success in these fields that his works and way of thinking, which integrated philosophy, religious jurisprudence and the principles of jurisprudence, have formed the foundation of a distinctive new school of investigative examination, creative opinion and methodology. In my opinion, the depth and novelty of ideas that the Martyr Imām put forward – especially compared with the traditional ways of thinking that characterized Islamic studies for so long – have slowed down their incoporation into the mindset of classical religious institutions and their dominance in the area of higher Islamic studies. However, his ideas have begun to make substantial inroads into the thinking of the religious intelligentsia; no doubt the al-Ṣadr school of thought, with its ideas and innovative approach, will ultimately prevail in Islamic scholarship.

The most important of his practical achievements can be summarized thus:

a) Nurturing highly moralistic and knowledgeable cadres, both inside and outside the Islamic seminaries. This has had a great impact on guiding the Islamic movement and educating and directing the *umma*'s various sections.

b) Insulating the minds of Muslim intellectuals from the onslaught of Western atheism, which has clothed itself in the garb of temptation and influence, such as the huge media empire that has swept the world, both East and West, and its scientific and technological capability that dominates the world's capitals and affects the political process and decision-making worldwide. Western ideology also holds sway over scientific and cultural institutions and achieves its overwhelming influence by virtue of its enormous financial and economic clout.

c) Establishing an Islamic activist organization, which is considered a qualitative step in the progress of Islamic resurgence within the Shiʿite domain.

d) Setting up the administrative arm of the guided religious authority (*marjaʿiyyah*) along on the lines discussed in his treatise on 'the good religious authority'. However, he did not hold the title of 'religious authority' for long, no more than ten years, as his reputation spread widely only in the last five years before his martyrdom, nor did it spread widely enough to enable him to achieve the goals he set out to achieve. In this he was thwarted by competing religious authorities, deeply rooted and with a large following and a long history, which attempted to prevent his religious authority from gaining any wider following. Additionally, the ruling Baʿth regime in Iraq was exercising pressure by various means in its attempt to hinder his religious authority, so as not to allow it to spread among the general populace (*umma*); among the regime's tactics was the arrest of his representatives in different parts of the country and the imposition of strict surveillance on those who were cooperating with or connected to his religious authority.

e) Setting forth the Islamic revolution in Iraq, leading it from the front and ensuring its continuity through his heroic steadfastness in the face of ferocious tyrants, even up to the time of his martyrdom.

Mohsen Araki

Foreword

'Ilm al-uṣūl (the science of the principles of jurisprudence) developed in the bosom of *'ilm al-fiqh* (the science of jurisprudence) just as the latter developed in the bosom of *'ilm al-hadīth* (the science of traditions), in accordance with the stages traversed by the science of the *Sharī'ā*.[1] By the science of the *Sharī'ā* we mean the science that endeavours to gain knowledge of the laws brought by Islam from Allah the Most High. This science began in the earliest part of Islamic history with the efforts of a large number of narrators to preserve and collect the traditions relevant to the laws of the *Sharī'ā*. Thus in the first stage the science of the *Sharī'ā* was at the level of *'ilm al-ḥadīth*. The basic task consisted almost entirely of collecting the traditions and preserving their texts. Determining a method of understanding the laws embodied in those texts and traditions was not particularly important at that stage, for it did not go beyond the simple method used by people to understand one another's words in everyday conversation.

Gradually the method of understanding the laws of *Sharī'ā* from the texts became more and more complex, until the derivation of laws from their sources became a precise and delicate matter, demanding profound and expert knowledge. Continually increasing efforts were made to acquire the precision required by the understanding of the laws of the *Sharī'ā* and their derivation from the sources. Thus the seeds of scientific legal thought

1. As a matter of convenience, the term *uṣūl* will be used in this book to denote *'ilm uṣūl al-fiqh* in order to avoid the cumbersome expression 'the science of the principles of jurisprudence'. Similarly, 'jurisprudence' will be used as a translation of *'ilm al-fiqh*.

developed and the science of jurisprudence was born. The science of the *Sharīʿā* thus ascended from the level of the science of tradition to that of deduction and precise scholarly reasoning.

In the course of the growth and development of jurisprudence, marked by a growing interest on the part of the scholars in the process of deduction, the common elements in that process of deduction began to manifest themselves. The practitioners of jurisprudence began to perceive the existence of common elements in the process of deduction without which that process could not take place. This signalled the birth of *uṣūl* and the acquisition by the legal mind of a methodological orientation.

Thus we can say that the science of the principles of *uṣūl* came into existence in the bosom of jurisprudence. Those engaged in the practice of jurisprudence were already using the common elements involved in the process of deduction without being fully aware of their nature, definition and importance in the process. Once methodological thought took hold, they became conscious of those elements and began to study their nature.

The seeds of that mode of thought were undoubtedly present among the jurists who were the companions of the Imāms from the time of Imāms Muḥammad Bāqir and Jaʿfar Ṣādiq (AS) onwards. Historical evidence to that effect is provided by the questions related in the books of *hadīth* concerning some of the common elements in the process of deduction, questions posed by a number of narrators to Imām Ṣādiq and other Imāms and answered by them. Those questions reveal the existence of the seeds of *uṣūli* thinking among them and of a tendency to establish general laws and delineate common elements. This view is strengthened by the fact that some of the companions of the Imāms wrote treatises on some of the problems of *uṣūl*. Thus Hisham b. al-Ḥakam wrote a treatise on terms (*al-alfāẓ*).

However, the concept of common elements and of the significance of their role in the process of deduction was not yet sufficiently clear or adequately developed. The elucidation and elaboration of their characteristics took place gradually during the expansion of jurisprudential activity and the development of the processes of deduction. The study of these common elements did not become a separate study, independent of jurisprudence, until long after the birth of the first seeds of methodological thinking. Thus the study of *uṣūl* remained for a long time intermingled with jurisprudence and it was neither studied nor written on as a subject in its own right. At the same time, *uṣūli* thinking was becoming continuously richer and its role increasingly clear until it reached a level at which it could become independent of jurisprudence.

Until then, *uṣūl* had continued to waver between jurisprudence and *'ilm uṣūl al*-dīn (the science of the creedal principles of religion). Thus sometimes discussions on *uṣūl al-fiqh* were mingled with discussions on *uṣūl al*-dīn and *kalām* (scholastic theology). Sayyid Murtaḍā indicates this in *al-Dharī'ah*, his book on *uṣūl al-fiqh*: 'I am aware of one who devoted a book to *uṣūl al-fiqh*. Although his detailed presentation of the meaning of that science, its principles and bases was highly accurate, he strayed way beyong the bounds of *uṣūl al-fiqh* and its methods. Thus he discussed the definitions of knowledge and speculation; how the latter may lead to the former; how effect necessarily follows from cause, as well as other matters, which belong entirely and exclusively to the domain of *uṣūl ad-din*, not to that of *uṣūl al-fiqh*.'

Similarly, we find that the independence of *uṣūl* as the science of the common elements in the process of deduction to derive the laws of the *Sharī'ā*, its separation from all other religious sciences including jurisprudence and *kalām*, came about only when the concept of the common elements and the necessity of formulating a general system for them had fully become clear. This was the factor which helped to distinguish studies in *uṣūl* from studies in jurisprudence and *kalām*, leading to the foundation of a separate science called *'ilm al-uṣūl*.

In spite of the fact that *uṣūl* was able to gain complete independence from *kalām*, there remained in it some conceptual residue, the history of which goes back to the time when the two sciences were intermingcd. This residue continued to be a source of confusion. Part of it was the concept that the narrations termed *akhbār āḥād* (suppositional narrations of unknown veracity) cannot be used as proofs in *uṣūl*, for every proof used in *uṣūl* has to be definite and decisive. The source of this concept is *kalām*, because the scholars of this science had ruled that the *uṣūl al*-dīn (the creedal principles of Islam) require definite and decisive proofs; we cannot establish the Attributes of Allah or the Hereafter on the basis of *akhbār āḥād*. The mingling of *uṣūl ad*-dīn with *uṣūl al-fiqh* and the fact that the names of both sciences contain the word *uṣūl* led to a generalization of this concept and its application to *uṣūl al-fiqh*. Thus we see that the books on *uṣūl al-fiqh* down to the time of Muḥaqqiq Ḥillī in the seventh century AH continued to object to the use of *akhbār āḥād* as a proof of the common elements in the process of deduction; they regarded it as a deviation from the above concept.

The book *al-Dhari'a*, when discussing the intermingling of *uṣūl al-fiqh* with *uṣūl al-dīn*, offers some fairly precise and well-defined observations about the common elements involved in the process of deduction. The author writes: 'Know that the discussions of *uṣūl al-fiqh* are in reality discussions about the proofs to be used in jurisprudence ... In view of what we have described, it is not necessary that the proofs and the methods of arriving at the laws and the branches of jurisprudence found in the books of the jurists be themselves in the nature of *uṣūl*, because the discussions on *uṣūl al-fiqh* relate to the evidentiary nature of the proofs by which these *uṣūl* establish laws, in general, not detailed fashion. The proofs of the jurists relate to the same pattern. Discussions of a general type are different from those that are detailed in nature.'

This quotation taken from one of the earliest sources on *uṣūl* in the Shi'ah heritage clearly includes the concept of the common elements in the process of deduction, calling them 'the proofs of *fiqh* (*adillat al-fiqh*) in general'. It makes a distinction between the subject-matter of *uṣūl* and that of jurisprudence on the basis of the distinction between the proofs of a general nature and those of a detailed nature, i.e. between the common elements and the specific elements, to use our terminology. This means that the concept of common elements had developed to a considerable degree by that time. It is found later in the writings of Shaykh Ṭūsī , Ibn Zuhrah, Muḥaqqiq Hillī and others. They all knew *uṣūl* to be 'the science of the proofs of *fiqh* in general', and attempted to express this by means of the concept of common elements.

In *Kitāb al-'uddah*, Shaykh Ṭūsī says: 'The *uṣūl al-fiqh* are the proofs of *fiqh*. Thus, when we discuss these proofs, we discuss in general fashion categories such as obligation, recommendation, permissibility, etc. It is not necessary for these proofs also to lead to the branches of *fiqh*, for they are proofs leading to the delineation of problems. Discussions of a general type are different from those specific or detailed in nature.' Here the terms 'general' and 'detailed' are used to denote the common and the specific elements respectively.

From the preceding we reach the conclusion that the emergence of *uṣūl*, of scholarly attention to the common elements in the process of deduction, depended both on the development of this process to a greater degree of precision and elaboration and on a deepening of legal thinking. It was no coincidence that *uṣūl* emerged later than *'ilm al-fiqh* and *'ilm al-hadīth*. Likewise, it was natural that *uṣūl* should develop in the bosom of *'ilm al-fiqh* after legal thinking had grown and developed to an extent that permitted the observation of the common elements and their scientific study. It was also natural that the concept of common elements should develop gradually and become more precise with the passage of time, until it gained its distinct form and precise contours, thereby becoming distinct from both *fiqh* and *uṣūl al-dīn*.

The Historical Necessity for Uṣūl

The delay in the emergence of *uṣūl*, after the appearance of *'ilm al-fiqh* and *'ilm al-ḥadīth*, was not simply the result of the connection between the outlook embodied in *uṣūl* and a relatively advanced level of legal thinking. Another point of great significance is that *uṣūl* did not exist as some kind of intellectual luxury, being instead the expression of an urgent need for the process of deduction, a process for which *uṣūl* was required to supply the indispensable common elements. The need for *uṣūl* arose from the need of the process of deduction for the common elements that are studied and delineated in this science. This need of the process of deduction for the common elements was not an absolute necessity; it arose as a historical need, a need that grew the more distant jurisprudence became from the period in which the texts were promulgated. It did not exist to the same degree in the jurisprudence of that period.

To understand this concept clearly, suppose that you were living in the time of the Prophet (SAWA), in close proximity to him, and that you used to hear the laws directly from him and fully understand the texts issued by him, thanks to their clarity of language and your direct acquaintance with the relevant contexts and circumstances. Would you then have needed, in order to understand the laws of the *Sharī'ā*, to have recourse to a common element of *uṣūl*, such as the validity of a narration as a proof, bearing in mind that you either heard the texts directly from the Prophet (SAWA) himself (peace be upon him) or they were transmitted to you by persons whom you knew directly and in whose truthfulness you had no doubt? Or would you have needed to refer to a common element of *uṣūl* like the evidentiary value of *al-zuhur al-'urfi* (apparent meaning as determined by conventional usage), when you were directly hearing the texts promulgated by the Prophet (SAWA) and clearly understanding the meaning he intended, without any doubt at all, thanks to your awareness of all the relevant circumstances and contexts? Or would you have needed to reflect on the formulation of laws for interpreting general statements issued by the Prophet (SAWA), even though you were in a position to ask him and seek clarification from him, thus removing all doubts?

What is implied by these questions is, of course, that the closer one is to the period in which the *Sharī'ā* was promulgated and the more intimately conversant with the texts, the less one needs to reflect on general laws and common elements. In that early period the deduction of the laws of the *Sharī'ā* took place in a simple manner, without jurists confronting numerous gaps that needed solution by means of the elements expounded in *uṣūl*. But as the jurists became ever more distant from the age in which the texts were issued and were forced to rely on historians, narrators and the traditionists for the transmission of the texts, they faced many gaps. They were thus compelled to contemplate the formulation of rules for filling those gaps. They asked: 'Was the transmitted text in reality given by the Ma'sūm to whom it is attributed or did the narrator lie? Did he perhaps make a mistake in transmitting it? What did the Ma'sūm mean by this text? Did he indeed intend the meaning I understand from the text when I read it or did it contain some other meaning, according to the circumstances and contexts in which it was issued and of which we are not aware? What does a jurist do when he is unable to find a text on a specific problem?' It is in this way that one comes to need aids such as the evidentiary validity of a *khabar* or of the apparent meaning of conventional usage, these being among the rules developed by *uṣūl*.

This is what we mean by saying that the need for *uṣūl* was historical in nature and separated in time from the age, circumstances and contexts in which the *Sharī'ā* was promulgated. It is this separation in time that accounts for the gaps that are encountered in the process of deduction. These gaps created an urgent need for *uṣūl* and its rules.

The pioneers of this science clearly understood this. That great sayyid, Hamza b. 'Alī b. Zahrah al-Ḥusaynī al-Ḥalabī (d. 585), wrote in the first chapter of his book *al-Ghunyah*:

'Since all discourse on the branches of jurisprudence is based on the principles [*uṣūl*] that are proper to it, it is essential to begin with those principles before pursuing the branches of jurisprudence. Any discussion of the branches without mastery of the *uṣūl* will not be fruitful.' Some opponents objected to this assertion, saying: 'If you act with respect to the *Sharī'ā* only on the basis of a statement of a Ma'sūm, what need do you have for *uṣūl*? Your discussions of it seem empty and useless.' In this passage, Ibn Zuhrah connects the need for *uṣūl* to the gaps that exist in the process of deduction, for he makes the commitment of the Imāmiyyah to following the pronouncements of the Ma'sūm the sole reason for any objection to his statement. In other words, as long as they continue following those pronouncements, they have no need for *uṣūl*. This is because, if the derivation of a law is based directly on a statement by the

Ma'sūm , it is a simple task, containing no gaps that might need to be filled by the formulation of the rules and elements of *uṣūl*.

In a passage of Muḥaqqiq Sayyid Muḥsin A'raji's (d. 1227 AH) *Wasa'il al-Shi'a* we find a complete awareness that *uṣūl* arose out of historical necessity. He speaks of the difference between those who were close to the age in which the texts were promulgated and those who are far removed from it, in context and circumstance. He remarks in this connection: 'What comparison is there between one favoured with nearness and one afflicted by distance, so that they can be termed equals in riches and poverty? No, they are as far apart as the heavens and the earth. What has befallen us because of the length of the Occultation, the severity of the hardships and the universality of the tribulations to which we are exposed would have thrown us back into Jāhiliyyah, had it not been for Allah and the blessings of His pious servants. Words have been corrupted, terminologies and usages have changed, contextual circumstances have disappeared, lies have increased, dissimulation has become widespread and contradictions between proofs have intensified, to the degree that one can barely find a single ruling that is universally agreed upon, because of all the differences to which it gives rise. At the same time there is also no one to whom questions may be addressed. One measure among others of the distinction between the two groups, early and late, is the difference in their circumstances and the fact that one expresses itself with confidence, the other with hesitation ... [The situation that pertained close to the time time of promulgation of the texts] is quite different from that of one who is obliged to deal with divergent narrations and contradictory traditions and must measure them against the Qur'ān and the known Sunnah. For such an individual preparation, readiness and practice are necessary to prevent error, because he has to select from among conflicting views.'

We thus realize that the delay in the historical emergence of *uṣūl* resulted not only from its connectedness with the development of legal thinking and the growth of deduction, but also from the nature of the need that gave rise to it. The need was historical and grew in proportion to chronological distance from the age in which the texts were promulgated.

Works on Uṣūl

The preceding enables us to explain the separation in time between the evolution of *uṣūl* among Sunni jurists and its evolution in the sphere of

Imāmī legal thinking. History indicates that this branch of knowledge thrived and flourished in the Sunni realm earlier than it did among Imāmī jurists. It is said that Sunni works on *uṣūl* began to be written towards the end of the second century (AH), examples being books written on the subject by al-Shāfi 'i (d. 189 AH) and Muḥammad b. Ḥasan al-Shaybānī (d. 189 AH). By contrast, no extensive work on the subject by a Shiʿite author is to be encountered until the years following the Lesser Occultation, i.e., the beginning of the fourth century Hijri. There are, however, some treatises on miscellaneous topics of *uṣūl* written by companions of the Imāms.

We have seen that the development of *uṣūli* thinking was the result of the need for principles in the sphere of deduction; that this need was historical; and that it grew and intensified as the distance in time increased from the age in which the texts were promulgated. It was therefore only natural that there should be separation in time between the Sunni and the Shi'a developments and that Sunni thinking on *uṣūl* should be the first to develop and expand, for the Sunni school of thought claims that the age of the promulgation of texts ended with the death of the Prophet (SAWA). Thus by the time that Sunni legal thinking reached the second century, it had become separated from the age of the promulgation of texts by a long period of time, which by its very nature had created gaps in the process of deduction. A pressing need was therefore felt for the formulation of the general rules of *uṣūl* to fill in the gaps. As regards the Imāmīs, they were at the time still living in the age of the promulgation of *Sharīʿā* texts, thanks to the presence among them of the Imām as a prolongation of the presence of the Prophet (SAWA). Thus the difficulties faced by the Imāmī jurists in making deduction were so few as to exclude all urgent necessity for formulating *uṣūl*.

For the Imāmīs, the age of the promulgation of texts ended with the beginning of the Occultation or more particularly with the end of the Lesser Occultation. It was only then that their thinking on *uṣūl* began to emerge and that they started studying the common elements in the process of deduction. Progress was accomplished in this field by a number of distinguished pioneers among the jurists, such as Hasan b. 'Alī b. Abī 'Aqīl and Muḥammad b. Aḥmad b. Junayd al-Iskāfī in the fourth century Hijri. *Uṣūl* then swiftly entered the stage of literary production. Shaykh Muḥammad b. Muḥammad b. Nuʿmānī known as Shaykh al-Mufīd (d. 413 AH) wrote a treatise on *uṣūl* in which he continued the line of thought followed by his predecessors, Ibn Abi 'Aqīl and Ibn Junayd, while criticizing them for a number of their views. Next came his pupil Sayyid

Murtaḍā (d. 436 AH), who developed further the same line of thinking on *uṣūl* and produced a relatively comprehensive work on the subject called *al-Dharī'ah*. In the preface Sayyid Murtaḍā affirmed that his work was unique in its comprehensive treatment of the distinctive trends of *uṣūl* prevailing among the Imāmīs.

Sayyid Murtaḍā was not the only one of the pupils of Shaykh Mufīd to have pursued the development of this new science and written on the subject. A number of others also wrote on *uṣūl*, among them Sallār b. 'Abd al-'Aziz al-Daylami (d. 436 AH), author of *al-Taqrīb fi uṣūl al-fiqh*. Another was the jurist Shaykh Muḥammad b. Ḥasan Ṭūsī (d. 460 AH), who was recognized as the leader of the jurists after Shaykh Mufīd and Sayyid Murtaḍā. He wrote a book on *uṣūl* called *al-'Uddah*. Thanks to his efforts *uṣūl* entered a new phase of intellectual maturity, just as, thanks to him, jurisprudence also attained a higher level of expansion and elaboration.

In addition to research and studies on *uṣūl*, an extensive effort was undertaken in the same age to collect the traditions transmitted from the Imāms of the Prophet's Household (AS) and to merge small collections of traditions into larger, comprehensive ones. By the that age had come to an end, Imāmī thinking had at its disposal the four comprehensive sources of traditions: *al-Kāfī* by Thiqat al-Islam Muḥammad b. Ya'qūb al-Kulayni (d. 329 AH); *Man la Yahḍuruhu 'l-Faqīh* by Shaykh al-Ṣadūq Muḥammad b. 'Alī b. al-Ḥusayn (d. 381 AH); *al-Tahdhīb* by Shaykh al-Ṭūsī , which he wrote during the lifetime of Shaykh al-Mufīd; and *al-Istibṣār*, also by Shaykh al-Ṭūsī . In Imāmī terminology, these books are called *al-Kutub al-arba'a* ('The Four Books').

Shaykh Ṭūsī's Development of the Sciences of Theory and Application

Shaykh al-Ṭūsī's contribution to *uṣūl* was not a continuation of the previous line of thinking. Rather, it represented a new development, which was part of an overall development in both juristic and scholarly thought. This pioneering jurist's book *al-'Uddah* reflected this development in the field of *uṣūl*, while his book *al-Mabsūṭ fi'l-fiqh* represented the same new stage of development in jurisprudence; the two works, representing theory and application respectively, thus complemented each other.

Shaykh al-Ṭūsī can be considered to embody the qualitative distinction between the tendencies resulting from this new development and those preceding it; his work serves as the line of demarcation between the era of preparation and that of maturity. He brought the preparatory era to a close and initiated the era of maturity, a period in which both jurisprudence and *uṣūl* became sciences with their own specific criteria, methods and modes of scholarly precision.

Within the limits of the present work, the best way to elucidate the great development in knowledge that occurred at the hands of Shaykh al-Ṭūsī will be to examine two statements by him, one in the introduction to *al-'Uddah* and the other in the introduction to *al-Mabsūṭ*. In the first he writes: 'You have requested (may Allah grant you support) a short discussion of *uṣūl al-fiqh* encompassing briefly and concisely all the relevant topics, in accordance with the views of our school of thought and our principles. Whoever has written on this subject up until now has done so along the lines dictated by his own principles (*uṣūl*). None of our companions is known to have written on this subject except Shaykh Abu 'Abdillah in *al-Mukhtaṣar*. However he did not exhaust the subject and certain of his views must be regarded as deviant and in need of rectification and revision. Sayyid Murtaḍā (may Allah perpetuate his high rank!) has drawn attention to many of those deviant views in much of his oral instruction, but he has not written anything on this subject to which reference may be made or on which reliance may be placed. In your request you have said: 'It is essential to attach the greatest importance to this branch of knowledge because the whole of the *Sharī'ā* is based on it, and complete knowledge of any of its aspects cannot be had without mastering its principles (*uṣūl*). And whoever does not master the principles can indeed be a transmitter or a layman, but not a scholar.'

This passage from Shaykh al-Ṭūsī reflects the significance of the development of *uṣūl* that he undertook by means of his book *al-'Uddah*, and illustrates the distinctive stamp he left on the whole field by the theories he elaborated within the general framework of the Imāmī school of thought. It also demonstrates that Shaykh al-Ṭūsī was the first Imāmī scholar to write on *uṣūl* and that he wrote *al-'Uddah* – or at least began writing it – during the lifetime of Sayyid Murtaḍā, because in one sentence he prays for a long life for him. He was perhaps unaware at the time of Sayyid Murtaḍā's book *al-Dharī'ah*, for he states that he had not written any book on *uṣūl*. This must mean either that Shaykh al-Ṭūsī began his book before Sayyid Murtaḍā wrote *al-Dharī'ah* or that *al-Dharī'ah* had already been written but was not widely known or publicized at the time.

Shaykh al-Ṭūsī writes in *al-Mabsūṭ*, his great work on jurisprudence: 'I continue to hear a group of jurists from among our opponents, persons claiming specialization in the branches of *fiqh*, belittling the jurisprudence of our Imāmī companions. Declaring them deficient with respect to the study of the branches of jurisprudence and of specific problems, they accuse them of being no more than the exponents of 'insertion'. Those who reject *qiyās* [analogy] and *ijtihād* [independent reasoning], they say, are incapable of developing the branches of jurisprudence and addressing an abundance of specific problems, for both of these are dependent on the two principles of *qiyās* and *ijtihād*. Their statement simply reflects their ignorance of our school of thought and their failure to reflect on our principles. Were these critics to examine our traditions and our jurisprudence, they would realize that most of the legal problems they mentioned are to be found in our traditions deriving from the Imāms, the evidentiary value of whose statements is identical to those of the Prophet (SAWA); their force is either specific or general, explicit or implicit. And as for the majority of problems relating to the branches (*furū'*) of jurisprudence with which their books are replete, there is none that is neglected by our principles or absent from our school of thought. They are dealt with not by means of *qiyās* but by means of a method yielding certain knowledge which then makes appropriate action obligatory, whether it be a question of primary exemption (*barā'at al-aṣl*) or something else. In addition, most of the branches of jurisprudence are to be found in the texts transmitted from our companions. The number of specific problems has been needlessly multiplied by the jurists because of their habit of compounding problems one with the other, making them ever more subtle and complex, until many questions that are quite clear and well-known are made artificially obscure.

'For a long time I have had a keen desire to write a book covering the whole field, but a variety of circumstances interrupted me and a plethora of tasks preoccupied me. I was also discouraged by the lack of demand for such a book on the part of this group and their lack of interest in the subject. They had compiled the traditions using exact and explicit wording, so that if a problem were presented in different wording or interpreted in a manner other than the conventional, they would be astonished and bereft of understanding. Previously I had written the book *al-Nihāyah* in which I had discussed all that was reported by our companions in their writings, together with the principal and secondary problems they had discussed. I disposed the material in the order of the problems of *fiqh*, assembled traditions of similar content and arranged the sections in the order I did for reasons explained in the book. I did not attempt to develop multiple branches of the problems, to complicate the various categories to which they belong, to comment on the different questions or to reconcile the traditions of similar content. Instead I presented all or most of my material using familiar terminology so that none might shy away from it. At the end of my work I discussed, with the utmost conciseness, the main categories of devotional acts and their legal classification.'

The Period of Stagnation

Perhaps the best historical document describing that period is a passage by that outstanding jurist, Muḥammad b. Aḥmad b. Idris, who lived during it and played a major role in resisting the stagnation. He infused scholarly thinking with new life, as we shall soon see. He writes in the preface to al-Sarā'ir: 'When I saw the indifference of the people of this age towards knowledge of the *Sharī'ā* of Muḥammad and the laws of Islam, their sluggishness in seeking it, their hostility towards that which they do not know and their neglect of that which they do know; when I saw that even the elders of this age are overwhelmed by ignorance so that they squander what the passage of days has deposited with them and neglect all knowledge except the obligatory, being concerned with only the present day, or even the present hour; and when I saw that the reins of knowledge were in the hands of those who were sinking to the depths of degradation and the field of knowledge was devoid of security, I took the necessary steps to preserve the remaining signs of life, and restored life, which was at the point of cessation.'

Renewal of Life and Vitality in Academic Research

Not a hundred years passed before new life was injected into Shi'ite scholarship on jurisprudence and its principles, at a time when Sunni scholarship remained as stagnant al-Ghazzālī had described it to be in the fifth century Hijri. A number of factors contributed to this difference, by means of which Shi'ite research regained its vigour in these fields in contrast to corresponding Sunni endeavours. We mention the following two:

The spirit of *taqlīd* (following or imitation). Although this spirit pervaded the academic circle left behind by Shaykh al-Ṭūsī just as it had permeated Sunni jurisprudence, its nature differed in the two cases. In the first case, the spirit of *taqlīd* dominated the circle left behind by Shaykh al-Ṭūsī because it had not yet matured and could not readily interact with his new and original ideas. Time needed to pass before that circle could fully grasp those ideas and interact with them or influence them. The spirit of *taqlīd* was, therefore, only temporary in this case. On the other hand, the spirit of *taqlīd* spread in Sunni juristic circles because there the discipline had fallen prey to old age; the limit of expansion had been reached and the objectives had been attained. We cannot elaborate on this point in the present context. However, it was only natural that the spirit of stagnation and *taqlīd* should become more firmly implanted in Sunni groups with the passage of time.

Sunni jurisprudence was the official jurisprudence adopted and consulted by the state insofar as it was committed to the fulfilment of its religious obligations. Thus the state provided impetus for the development of Sunni jurisprudence. However, this meant that Sunni jurisprudence was influenced by political circumstances, flourishing in times of political stability and losing its lustre whenever political confusion reigned.

It was therefore only natural that Sunni jurisprudence should forfeit much of its vitality in the sixth and seventh centuries and afterwards as a result of the political instability that culminated in the devastation wrought on the Muslim world by the Mongols.

By contrast, Imāmī jurisprudence was always separate from the state and frequently subject to oppression by its organs. The Imāmīs did not derive their motivation for scholarly work from the needs of the ruling institution, but from the needs of people who believed in the Imām ate of the Household of the Prophet (SAWA) and who had recourse to the jurists of this school to solve their religious problems and to ascertain their obligations according to the *Sharī'ā*. Thus Shi'ite jurisprudence was influenced by the needs of the people, not by the political environment as was the case with Sunni jurisprudence.

In addition, the Shi'a, devoted as they were to practising their religion according to the jurisprudence of the Household of the Prophet (SAWA), were constantly growing in number, and they had therefore increasing occasion to consult their jurists for authoritative rulings. This enables us to understand how, far from forfeiting factors of growth, Shi'ite jurisprudence expanded together with the expansion of Shi'ism itself and with the spread of the idea of *taqlīd* , in the sense of following the rulings of a qualified jurist. Shi'ite scholarly thinking possessed both internal factors of expansion – its relative youth and capacity for development – and external –the ties linking the Imāmī jurists to the Shi'a community with its increasing needs. The relative stagnation of Shi'ite jurisprudence after the death of the illustrious Shaykh Ṭūsī can be said to have served the purpose of gathering its forces in preparation for further development and growth to a point where it could interact with his views.

The element of motivation possessed by Sunni scholarly thought – government patronage – was absent among the Shiʿites, where a degree of stagnation also prevailed in teaching circles. The propagation of Shiʿism, however, endowed Shiʿi thought with new vitality. This activity was particularly marked from the seventh century Hijri onwards, and it was undertaken by scholars such as ʿAllamah Hilli . This in itself endowed Shiʿite scholarly thinking with greater depth, in part the result of studying the *uṣūl*, jurisprudence and *kalām* of the Sunnis. Scholars such as ʿAllāmah Ḥillī who were involved in this propagation of Shiʿism engaged to a remarkable degree in studies of comparative jurisprudence.

LESSON ONE

Definition of the Science of Jurisprudence (*Fiqh*)

After an individual has established faith in God, Islam and the revealed law (*Sharī'ā*) and understands that, as a servant of God, he must obey His revealed laws, it becomes necessary for him to make his conduct, in different fields of life, conform to the *Sharī'ā*. He does this by adopting the practical stance that is necessitated by his submission to the *Sharī'ā*; it is crucial for him to determine this in order to know how to discharge his duties in every circumstance.

Defining such a practical stance in the context of the *Sharī'ā* would be easy for everyone if the rules of the *Sharī'ā* in every case were clear and evident. There would then be no need for scholarly discussions and arduous studies of the matter. However, numerous factors such as our remoteness in time from the legislative era have led to a lack of clarity in a number of legal rulings, and this has covered them in shrouds of ambiguity.

It was therefore essential to establish a science that would set out to eliminate such ambiguities by furnishing proof or evidence (*dalīl*) for determining the practical stance to be adopted in each case. The science of jurisprudence (*fiqh*) came into being in order to assume precisely this task. It defines the practical stance to be adopted in regard to the *Sharī'ā* by adducing the relevant evidence. This is what we call the procedure for the derivation of a *shar'i* ruling. We can therefore define the science of jurisprudence as the science of the derivation of *shar'i* rulings or as the science of the procedure by which that derivation takes place.

The determination of the practical stance by means of evidence takes place in one of the following two ways: by specifying the relevant ruling of the *Sharīʿā* or by specifying what is to be done when no ruling is or can be known.

The material on which the first method draws consists of what is known as 'the evidences' (*al-adillah*) or more fully as 'the securing proofs' (*al- adillah al-muhrizah*) because they make it possible to 'secure' the *sharʿi* ruling. That employed in the second method consists of what is known as 'the procedural proofs' (*al-adillah al-ʿamaliyyah*) or 'the procedural principles' (*al-uṣūl al-ʿamaliyya*). Whichever method he employs, the goal of the jurist is to establish the practical stance to be adopted in a given situation.

Despite the number and variety of the procedures of derivation that are involved in the science of jurisprudence (*fiqh*), they share certain unifying elements and general principles. The study of those elements necessitated the formation of a specialized science devoted to defining and preparing them for use in the science of jurisprudence. This specialized branch of knowledge came to be known as the science of the principles of jurisprudence (*uṣūl al-fiqh*).

LESSON TWO

Definition of the Science of the Principles of Jurispudence (*Uṣūl*)

The science of *uṣūl* can then be defined as the science of the common elements that are used in the procedure of derivation of a *shar'ī* ruling.

In order to do justice to this definition, we must understand what these common elements are. We will therefore provide some elementary examples of the procedure of derivation and compare their common elements.

Let us suppose a jurist is faced with the following three questions:

1. Is it forbidden for an individual who is fasting to immerse his head in water?

2. Is it obligatory for an individual who has inherited property from his father to pay *khums* on it?

3. Does guffawing during a prayer invalidate it?

The jurist will answer the first question in the affirmative, basing his ruling on a tradition from Imām al-Ṣādiq (upon whom be peace), narrated by Ya'qub b. Shu'ayb, to the effect that immersion of the head in water while fasting is forbidden. The Imām said: 'Neither the one in a state of consecration for *ḥajj* nor the one who fasts may immerse his head in water.' A sentence using the negative form of the verb in this fashion indicates prohibition according to general usage. The narrator of the text is, moreover, a trustworthy person (*thiqah*); and although a trustworthy person may sometimes appear to err or deviate from the norm, the Legislator has instructed us not to accuse him of error or lying. Indeed, the report of such a person is considered to be authoritative (*ḥujjah*). Hence the conclusion that immersing one's head in water while fasting is prohibited.

The jurist will answer the second question in the negative, basing himself on a tradition narrated by 'Alī ibn Mahziyār, which defines the types of property that are subject to the *khums*. The tradition specifies that *khums* is not to be levied on an inheritance passing from father to son or vice versa, from which it is concluded, in accordance with the normal sense of the words employed, that the Legislator has not imposed the payment of *khums* in such cases. The narrator in this case is again trustworthy, and the same considerations mentioned in the previous case apply here also. Hence the conclusion that the payment of *khums* on an estate of inherited from one's father is not obligatory.

The jurist answers the third question in the affirmative, basing himself on a tradition of Imām al-Ṣādiq (upon whom be peace), narrated by Ḍurarah , to the effect that 'guffawing does not invalidate ablution but it does invalidate prayer'. The normal sense of the words used here clearly indicate that prayer is invalidated in such circumstances, and Ḍurarah , the person narrating them, is trustworthy. Hence the obvious conclusion reached by the jurist.

The rulings given by our jurist in answer to these three questions related to different areas of concern (*abwāb*) of jurisprudence, and the evidence that he relied on in each case was also different – different traditions related by three different persons. Each of the three traditions has its own text and linguistic structure, the meaning of which must be separately determined. Common elements are, however, seen to have been used by the jurist in all three cases. One of those elements is reference to normal linguistic usage in understanding utterances made by the Ma'sūm. This is termed the validity of the apparent meaning as determined by normal usage (*ḥujjiyyat al-ẓuhūr al-'urfī*). Another common element is the authority of a tradition narrated by a trustworthy person.

The process of derivation thus incorporates common elements as well as specific elements that vary from one case to another. The tradition narrated by Ya'qūb b. Shu'ayb is a specific element used in deriving the unlawfulness of immersion, but not in the two other procedures of derivation, where the specific elements are the traditions narrated by 'Alī b. Mahziyār and Ḍurārah respectively. The common elements are those general principles to which recourse is had in deriving rulings related to all the different areas of concern of jurisprudence.

The common elements form the subject matter of the science of *uṣūl* and the specific elements pertaining to each individual case are the subject matter of the science of jurisprudence (*fiqh*). It is thus the duty of the jurist to study carefully, in each instance, the traditions and other sources that are specifically connected to it. He also studies the value of those traditions, and endeavours to comprehend the meaning of their verbal content, their apparent meaning according to normal usage and their chains of transmission. The scholar of *uṣūl* concerns himself, by contrast, with questions such as the authority of the apparent meaning of a tradition as determined by normal usage (*ḥujjiyyat al-ẓuhūr*) and the authority of the tradition itself (*ḥujjiyyat al-khabar*).

In addition to defining the common elements, the science of *uṣūl* defines the ways in which they may be used and the relationships that exist between them. We will deal with all this in the lessons that follow, God willing.

A science usually has an essential subject matter on which all its topics are centred; the aim is to discover the characteristics, particularities and laws that relate to the essential subject matter. The essential subject matter of physics, for example, is nature, and that of grammar is language, because it deals with inflections, conjugations and declensions.

What is the essential subject matter of the science of *uṣūl*? Bearing in mind the definition we provided above for this science, we can state that its essential subject matter consists of the common evidences that are used in the process of derivation and that the purpose of its studies is to establish the evidentiary value of these common evidences.

LESSON THREE

The Science of *Uṣūl*, the Logic of Jurisprudence

Our acquaintance with the science of logic permits us to use it as something of an analogue for the science of *uṣūl*. Logic studies the general procedures of reasoning, irrespective of the subject and discipline involved. It defines the general principles that must be observed for reasoning to be sound and teaches us how to advance an argument and make valid deductions. How, for example, do we deduce that Socrates is mortal? How do we prove that the fire in the hearth in front of me can burn? How do we deduce that the sum of the angles of a triangle is equal to two right angles? How do we argue that a continuous straight line without any end is impossible? The science of logic answers all of this by establishing universal methods for deduction, such as syllogism (*qiyās*) and induction (*istiqrā'*).

The science of *uṣūl* resembles the science of logic from this point of view, with the difference that it is devoted to a specific type of reasoning, namely, that involved in the derivation of *shar'i* rulings. *Uṣūl* studies the common elements that must be an integral part of that procedure for the reasoning underlying it to be sound. By establishing the common elements and general methods required for using them correctly, *uṣūl* teaches us how to conclude that immersion while fasting is unlawful; how to deduce that water up to the measure of a *kurr* is not susceptible to contamination; and how to decide whether *'Id* prayers are recommended or obligatory.

Uṣūl may therefore be designated as the logic of the science of jurisprudence, since its relationship to that science resembles the relationship of logic to general human reasoning.

There is no need to stress any further the importance of the science of *uṣūl* and the crucial role it plays in the procedure of derivation. Without this science, the practitioner of jurisprudence would find himself confronted with a scattered array of texts and evidences, totally unable to make use of them for the purpose of derivation. It would be like giving someone a saw, an axe and other tools, without his having a general idea of how to use them for the purposes of carpentry.

The specific elements are, however, no less essential to the procedure of derivation than are the common elements. They differ from one issue to another, examples being the wording of specific verses of the Qur'ān and traditions relevant to each issue. Acquaintance with the common elements examined in the science of *uṣūl* is insufficient for engaging in the procedure of derivation. Anyone who attempts to do so armed only with this knowledge would be like someone having some general notions about carpentry but lacking an axe and a saw. Such a person would certainly be unable to make a wooden bed, and analogously a scholar versed only in *uṣūl* would be unable to engage in the derivation of rulings.

Common elements and specific elements are therefore both indispensable to the procedure of derivation; they must be employed together in order to attain beneficial results.

We have said that in the science of *uṣūl* a jurist studies, defines and delineates the common elements, while in the science of jurisprudence he deals with the specific elements that, when added to the common elements, complete the process of legal deduction. This should not be taken to mean that if one studies the common elements of derivation and grasps principles such as the authoritative nature of single reports made by a trustworthy narrator and the apparent meaning of texts, no further scholarly exertion is required in order to complete the procedure of derivation. It is not the case that all that is needed is to extract the relevant traditions from their sources and then add them to the common elements, which would indeed be a fairly straightforward task.

After the jurist has identified the common elements established by the science of *uṣūl*, he needs to do more than blindly assemble the specific elements from books of tradition in order to begin applying them to the procedure of derivation. It will be his duty to examine the applicability of those common elements and the general theories underlying them to the specific issues at hand. Testing applicability is a separate skill in its own right, requiring long and careful study, beyond the general study of *uṣūl*. Let us suppose that from his study of *uṣūl* a jurist has become convinced that the apparent meaning of a word, as determined by normal usage, is authoritative. In order to reach the conclusion that *khums* is not payable on an estate left to a person by his father, it would not be enough for our jurist to point to the statement narrated by ʿAlī b. Mahziyār defining the types of property on which *khums* is to be levied and then add to it the relevant common elements. He would additionally need to examine closely the text of the report in order to discover what precisely is its apparent meaning in normal usage. He would also have to take into consideration contextual elements, both those in the text itself and those found elsewhere, that might have a bearing on the definition of the apparent meaning.

Bearng all this in mind, it is clear that the use of specific elements involved in procedures of derivation requires far more than a simple process of gathering and assembling; the applicability of the theories of *uṣūl* must also be examined, a task demanding specific skills in its own right. Precision is always needed both in the formulation of theories and in their application. A person who has mastered the general theories of medicine must acquaint himself precisely and in detail with the state of his patients before he ventures to apply his theories on them.

LESSON FOUR

Interaction Between Jurisprudence and *Uṣūl*

The science of *uṣūl* counts, then, as the logic specific to jurisprudence, and its relationship to it is that of theory to practice. This explains why there is interaction between the theoretical mode of thought involved in *uṣūl* and the practical mode of thought involved in jurisprudence. Advances in application always stimulate progress in theory, because the problems that emerge in the course of application call for theoretical solutions. Conversely, the refinement of legal theories is reflected at the level of application, because the more numerous and precise the theories become, the more complex and intricate becomes the task of application.

This interaction between the two modes of thought is observable throughout the history of both disciplines. *Uṣūl* grew out of the science of jurisprudence, just as that discipline had developed from the science of traditions. It was not, in fact, an independent science to begin with, distinct from the science of jurisprudence. But once jurisprudence started to develop, converging trends and common elements began to make themselves known, and the practitioners of jurisprudence began to recognize common elements shared by all procedures of derivation and essential to them.

This was the development that signalled the birth of the science of *uṣūl*. It gradually disengaged itself from the science of jurisprudence as a subject of research and writing, expanding as a result both of a growth in theoretical concepts of the legal theory and of an increase in practical issues of jurisprudence. As the scope of application widened, the jurists intensified their search for new and appropriate solutions, and these solutions took the form of the common elements, the basic substance of *uṣūl*.

The more distant the jurist became in time from the legislative era, the more numerous became the difficulties involved in understanding a *shar'i* ruling purely on the basis of its sources. The same factor caused various lacunae to arise in the procedure of derivation. A pressing need made itself felt for defining the general concepts that would enable these problems to be solved. The need for the science of *uṣūl* was then a historic one, in the sense that it became more urgent the greater the distance became between the jurist and the legislative era.

This enables us to explain the chronological gap between the development of *uṣūl* in Sunni legal thinking and in our Imāmī thinking. The earlier flourishing of *uṣūl* among the Sunnis was due to their belief that the legislative era had come to an end with the death of the Prophet (SAWA) (SAWA), so that by the close of the second century, they found themselves at a considerable distance from the legislative era and encumbered with a number of lacunae and obscurities.

By contrast, the Imāmīs were still living in the legislative era, for they considered the Imām to be an extension of the presence of the Prophet (SAWA). The difficulties experienced by Shi'i jurists were accordingly fewer, with the result that no pressing need was felt for a science of *uṣūl*. But no sooner did the legislative era come to an end for the Imāmiyyah with the beginning of the Occultation (or, more precisely, the end of the Minor Occultation) than they too began to take a greater interest in the science of *uṣūl* and the study of the common elements.

This does not mean, of course, that the seeds of *uṣūli* thinking were lacking among the jurists who were companions of the Imāms. Those seeds were indeed present during the Imām ates of Muḥammad al-Bāqir and Ja'far al-Ṣādiq, at a level appropriate to that particular phase. The evidence for this can be found in the books of Imāmī tradition where we read of questions relating to the common elements being brought to the attention of Imām al-Ṣādiq (pbuh) and other Imāms. We know, too, that some of the companions of the Imāms compiled treatises on questions of *uṣūl*, such as Hishām b. al-Ḥakam, a companion of Imām al-Ṣādiq , who is reported to have compiled a treatise on terminology (*al-alfāẓ*).

LESSON FIVE

The Permissibility of the Procedure of Deduction

Since the science of *uṣūl* deals with the deduction of *shar'i* rulings and defines the common elements involved, we must first ascertain the standpoint of the *Sharī'ā* on this procedure. Does the Legislator permit the practice of deduction, making it permissible for us establish a science to study its common elements?

When the issue is presented in this manner, it does not appear to call for debate, since it is self-evident that the answer is affirmative. The procedure of religious derivation, as previously stated, consists of defining, by means of evidence, the practical standpoint to be adopted with regard to the *Sharī'ā*, and it is obvious that every individual who is subject to the authority of the *Sharī'ā* needs to know that practical standpoint. Now, most *shar'i* rulings are not clear enough to be established without the adducing of evidence, and it would therefore be contrary to reason to consider such adducing of evidence unlawful.

Unfortunately, however, the issue was sometimes posed in terms of *ijtihād*, an expression that caused confusion and controversy when applied to the procedure of derivation. The question then became whether or not *ijtihād* is permissible with regard to the *Sharī'ā*. The word had been used to denote diverse meanings in its history, which cast a shadow over the debate. Some jurists answered the question about its permissibility in the negative, which led them to condemn the science of *uṣūl*, for *uṣūl* by its very nature is a discipline devoted to the practice of *ijtihād*.

To clarify what is at issue, we must review the various senses in which the word *ijtihād* has been used and the evolution it has undergone. *Ijtihād* is lexically derived from *juhd*, which means 'exerting the utmost effort in order to accomplish a certain action'. In jurisprudence this term was used by some Sunni schools of jurisprudence to denote one of the principles they followed. The principle is that whenever a jurist wishes to derive a *shar'i* ruling and cannot find a relevant text in the Qur'ān or the Sunnah, he should have recourse to *ijtihād*. In this context *ijtihād* means 'personal thinking, preference or opinion', and is identical to what is known as *ra'y* ('opinion'). *Ijtihād* thus comes to function as one of the proofs and sources of the jurist, like the Qur'ān and the Sunnah. It was espoused in this sense by major schools of Sunni jurisprudence, especially that founded by Abu Hanifa, a sense it retained until the seventh century.

This type of *ijtihād* was, however, bitterly opposed by the Imāms of the Household of the Prophet (SAWA) and the jurists affiliated to them. We find narrations transmitted from the Imāms condemning it and books being written against it by some of those who reported their traditions, examples being 'Abdullah b. 'Abd al-Rahman al- Zubayri's *al-Istifāda fi 'l-Tu'un 'ala 'l-Awā'il wa 'l Radd 'ala Aṣḥāb al-Ijtihād wa 'l-Qiyās* ('The Benefit in Criticizing the Predecessors and the Refutation of the Proponents of *Ijtihād* and Analogy'), and Hilal b. Ibrahim b. Abi al-Fatḥ al-Madani's *al-Radd 'ala man Radda Āthār al-Rasūl wa I'tamada 'ala Natā'ij al-'Uqūl* ('The Refutation of Those Who Reject the Traditions of the Prophet (SAWA) and Rely on the Results of Reason').

Similarly, al-Najashi, author of *al-Rijāl*, informs us that in the era of the Minor Occultation or thereabouts Isma'il b. 'Alī b. Ishaq b. Abi Sahl al-Nawbakhti wrote a book refuting the views of 'Isa b. Aban on *ijtihād*. The offensive was continued after the Minor Occultation, in the middle of the fourth century, by al-Ṣadūq . We mention here by way of example the comment he made on the story of Prophet Moses (AS) and al-Khidr: 'Despite the perfection of his intellect, his excellence and his rank in the view of God Almighty, Moses (AS) was unable to grasp the meaning of al-Khidr's actions by means of his reason and deduction, and thus remained in a state of confusion. If it is not permissible for the prophets and messengers of God to use analogical reasoning, deduction and derivation, it is still less appropriate for the rest of mankind to do so ... If Moses (AS) was not fit to exercise choice in the matter, despite his excellence and high rank in God's view, how can the *umma* be fit to choose its Imām or to deduce and derive *shar'i* rulings by having recourse to their deficient intellects and diverse opinions?'

At the close of the fourth century, al-Shaykh al-Mufid pursued the attack on *ijtihād*, understood in the sense outlined above, in his *al-Naqd 'ala ibn al-Junayd fi Ijtihād al-Ra'y* ('A Critique of Ibn al-Junayd for his Use of Personal Judgement'), and at the beginning of the following century al-

Sayyid al-Murtada wrote the following in his *al-Dharī'ah*: '*ijtihād* is invalid, and it is not permissible for the Imāmiyyah to base their practice on supposition (*zann*), personal opinion (*ra'y*) or *ijtihād*.' He also makes this criticism of Ibn al-Junayd in his *al-Intiṣār*, a book on jurisprudence: 'With regard to this issue Ibn al-Junayd has relied on a type of personal judgement and *ijtihād*, and this is a manifest error.' In the same book, in the chapter on purification, he writes, while discussing the wiping of the feet: 'We do not regard *ijtihād* as appropriate nor do we uphold it.'

This understanding of *ijtihād* continued to prevail for some time. Al-Shaykh al-Ṭūsī , who died in the middle of the fifth century, wrote the following in his *al-'Uddah*: 'We do not regard analogical reasoning and *ijtihād* as sources of evidence and recourse to them is prohibited in the *Sharī'ā*.' In *al-Sarā'ir*, written towards the end of the sixth century, Ibn Idris reviews a number of criteria for preferring one of two contradictory pieces of evidence. After identifying his chosen criterion, he writes: 'No other criterion exists, in the view of our companions; we hold analogical reasoning, personal preference (*istiḥsān*) and *ijtihād* all to be invalid.'

These texts indicate that the term *ijtihād* retained the meaning we have outlined down to the beginning of the seventh century, and it had a distasteful connotation for the Imāmī jurists. Its meaning evolved, however, in our juridical terminology. We find al-Muḥaqqiq al-Ḥillī (d. 676 AH) writing the following under the heading, 'the true nature of *ijtihād*' in his *al-Ma'ārij*: 'In the terminology of the jurists *ijtihād* means exerting the utmost effort in order to derive a ruling of the *Sharī'ā*. Indeed, the derivation of *shar'i* rulings from their sources is identical with *ijtihād*, for such derivation is based mostly on theoretical considerations which are not understood from the explicit meanings of the texts, whether the source be analogy or something else. Analogy is thus only one type of *ijtihād*. It may then be remarked that if this be the case, the Imāmīs accept *ijtihād*. To this I reply that indeed they do, although this is misleading insofar as analogy is a variety of *ijtihād*. I say therefore that we are proponents of *ijtihād* in the sense of deriving rulings by theoretical methods that do not include analogy.'

It is clear from this statement that for some people the term *ijtihād* continued to be encumbered with its old usage and that they therefore found it difficult to call the Imāmī jurists practitioners of *ijtihād*, i.e., *mujtahids*. Al-Muḥaqqiq al-Ḥillī , by contrast, was not at all disturbed by the word *ijtihād* once he had developed its meaning or, it would be better to say, once it had developed in the usage of Imāmī jurists in a way that made it compatible with their methods of derivation. *Ijtihād* had been a source from which the jurist could derive a *shar'i* ruling and a proof on which he could base his argument, just as was the case with a verse of the Qur'ān or a tradition of a Ma'sūm . In the new usage, it denoted 'to express the effort of the jurist to derive a *shar'i* ruling from its sources'; it was no longer regarded as one of the sources but as a procedure used to derive a ruling from the sources.

It is essential to understand the difference between the two meanings. According to the first, the jurist must derive a ruling from his personal thinking and private inclinations whenever he is faced with a lack of textual evidence. When questioned about the source of his ruling, he can justifiably reply that he has resorted to *ijtihād* and that is his source. The second meaning given to *ijtihād* would not permit him to give such an answer, because *ijtihād* is only a procedure, not a source. When a jurist says, in accordance with the second meaning, 'This is my *ijtihād*,' he means, in effect, 'This is what I have deduced from the authorized sources and accepted proofs,' and everybody has the right to question him about those sources and proofs.

The meaning of *ijtihād* was destined to undergo still further development. Al-Muḥaqqiq al-Ḥillī had limited its usage to the procedure of derivations that were not based on the apparent meanings of authoritative texts. Every procedure of derivation that went beyond the apparent textual meaning was therefore called *ijtihād*. The reason for this may have been that simple recourse to apparent meaning did not involve an effort great enough to qualify for the designation *ijtihād*. Later, however, the sense of the term did begin to include the procedures of derivation based on apparent meaning. For some scholars of *uṣūl* were of the opinion that that even the procedure of deriving a ruling from apparent meanings required considerable scholarly effort, including the understanding and definition of apparent meanings and proving the authoritative nature of conventional usage. The meaning of *ijithād* then expanded still further to include all kinds of derivations, aimed at establishing the practical standpoint to be adopted vis-à-vis the *Sharī'ā*.

The foregoing makes it possible to explain the attitude of a group of our respected scholars who have opposed the term *ijtihād*. Their opposition arose from the lingering effects of the former usage of the term, a usage that had been severely attacked by the Ahl al-Bayt and was entirely different from *ijtihād* in the sense that it later acquired. As long as we distinguish the two meanings of *ijtihād* from each other, the matter will be clear to us and we will understand *ijtihād* to be permissible in its sense of synonymity with the procedure of derivation. It follows that it is necessary to retain the science of *uṣūl* in order to study the common elements involved in the procedure of derivation.

LESSON SIX

Shar'i Rulings and Their Divisions

We have learned that the science of the principles of jurisprudence studies the common elements in the procedures for the derivation of a religious ruling. It is therefore necessary, before all else, to form a general concept of what precisely constitutes a religious ruling.

A *shar'i* ruling is an instance of legislation issuing from God, the Exalted, with the purpose of organizing the life of human beings. The revealed addresses (*al-khitābāt*) in the Qur'ān and the Sunnah are not considered to be religious rulings in themselves, although they disclose and shed light on religious rulings. In the light of this, it is incorrect to define a religious ruling with the well-known formula used by the earlier legal theorists: 'a legislative address concerning the actions of those held accountable by law (*al-mukallafūn*).' For the address merely discloses the ruling, the ruling itself being what is indicated by the address. In addition, the religious ruling is not always related to the actions of the accountable, for it is sometimes related to their persons or to other things connected to them. This is because the purpose of the religious rulings is to organize human life, and just as this objective is achieved through an address related to the actions of the accountable, such as 'pray', 'fast' or 'do not drink alcohol', it is also achieved by addresses related to their persons or other things connected to their lives. Examples of the latter category are addresses such as those organizing the matrimonial relationship by which, under specific conditions, a woman is considered a wife of a man, or the relationship involved in ownership, whereby a person is considered the owner of property. These rulings are not related to the actions of the legally accountable: matrimony relates to their persons and ownership relates to their property. Thus, it is better to change the popular form [of the definition] to what we said, namely: 'the religious ruling is the legislation issued from God, the Exalted, to organize human life, whether or not it is related to their [general] actions, to themselves or to other things related to their lives.

In the light of the foregoing it is possible to divide the religious ruling into two types.

First, rulings which are related to the actions of human beings and directly address their conduct in different aspects of personal, devotional, family and social life, all of which are dealt with and organized by the Sharīʿā. These include such rulings as the unlawfulness of consuming alcoholic beverages, the obligatoriness of prayer, the obligation to give financial support to certain close relatives, the permissibility of reviving neglected land and the obligation of rulers to act with justice.

Second, rulings which do not address human actions and conduct directly, but legislate for certain situations that have an indirect effect on human conduct, such as the rulings that regulate matrimonial relations. These rulings legislate in a direct manner a specific relationship between men and women, but affect and orient human conduct indirectly, because, for example, after the woman has become a wife, she must conduct herself in a specific manner with regard to her husband. Rulings of this type are called situational rulings (*al-aḥkām al-waḍʿiyyah*).

There is a strong connection between situational rulings and rulings of general obligation (*al-aḥkām al-taklīfiyyah*), since no situational ruling exists without one of general obligation existing alongside it. Matrimony, for example, is a situational ruling alongside which exist many rulings of general obligation, such as the obligation of the husband to support his wife and the obligation of the wife to grant him access to her person. Ownership is another situational ruling alongside which exist rulings of general obligation, such as the impermissibility of the use of property by a person other than the owner without his consent.

Rulings of general obligation fall into the following five categories:

Obligatoriness (*al-wujūb*): a ruling that impels a person towards the matter in question at the level of absolute requirement, examples being the performance of prayer and the making of provision for the destitute by the legitimate holder of authority.

Recommendation (*al-istiḥbāb*): a ruling that impels a person towards the matter in question at a level lower than obligatoriness. There always exists a dispensation (*rukhṣa*) from the Legislator to ignore the matter in question, an example being the performance of the night prayer.

Prohibition (*al-ḥurmah*): a ruling that restrains a person from the matter in question at the level of absolute obligation, examples being the taking of interest, fornication and adultery, and the selling of weapons to the enemies of Islam.

Reprehensibility (*al-kirāhah*): a ruling that restrains a person from the matter in question at a level not reaching that of absolute obligation. Hence, reprehensibility in the sphere of restraint corresponds to recommendation in the sphere of impelling, just as prohibition in the sphere of restraint is like obligatoriness in the sphere of impelling. An example of a reprehensible action is violating a promise.

Permissibility (*al-ibaḥah*): a ruling that arises whenever the Legislator grants those held accountable by law the opportunity to choose the stance he wishes to adopt with respect to a particular matter. The result is freedom to perform or omit a particular act.

LESSON SEVEN

Types of Derivative Procedure

When a jurist deals with an issue such as saying the *iqāmah* before prayer and tries to deduce its ruling, he will first ask himself what is the type of ruling that pertains to the matter. If he comes upon any evidence indicating the type, it is his duty to define his practical standpoint and his deduction on that basis. His derivation will then be one based on evidence.

However, if the jurist does not encounter such evidence, the ruling will remain unknown to him. In this situation, he will substitute a new question for the one he asked himself at the beginning: what are the principles that define the practical standpoint to be adopted in the case of an unknown religious ruling? These principles are called the practical principles (*al-uṣūl al-'amaliyyah*).

One example is the principle of original exemption (*aṣālat al-barā'ah*), which states that: 'Every unknown obligation or prohibition for which no evidence can be adduced has no effect on the conduct of a person, and he is not required to take precaution (*ihtiyāṭ*) with regard to it nor is he bound by it.' In such a case, derivation will be on the basis of a practical principle (*al-aṣl al-'amali*) instead of evidence.

The difference between the principle (*al-aṣl*) and the evidence (*al-dalīl*) is that the principle does not define the reality of the matter under consideration but only the practical duty towards it. It is nonetheless a type of derivation. We can therefore categorize the procedures of derivation as follows:

1. Derivation based on evidence (*al-dalīl*), like the derivation drawing on a text that indicates a legal ruling.

2. Derivation based on a practical principle, like the derivation that relies on the principle of original exemption.

The principles of jurisprudence constitute the science that studies the common elements for the procedure of derivation. It therefore includes in its scope the common elements that exist in both of these categories. It is on this basis that we divide juridical investigations into two types. Under the heading of the first type, we will explore the common elements in the procedure of derivation based on the securing evidences (*al-adillah al-muḥrizah*). Under the heading of the second type we will discuss the common elements in the procedure of derivation based on practical principles. In addition, there is a common element that includes all the other elements involved in both types of derivation. This is known as 'evidentiary certitude' (*ḥujjiyat al-qaṭ'*).

Since these elements and proofs may sometimes contradict each other, we must examine the methods available for solving the problem, and will do so at the end of the book.

Let us now take up the issue of 'evidentiary certitude'. 'Certitude' means in this context the exposition of an issue in a manner that leaves absolutely no room for doubt. The meaning of this certitude could be demonstrated in two situations:

1. When a believer disobeys his Lord as the result of an action arising from erroneous certitude and belief, it will not be fitting for the Lord to punish him. The believer could excuse his disobedience on the basis that he acted according to his certitude. An example would be a person mistakenly believing that the drink in front of him is not wine and drinking it relying on this certitude. The Lord will not punish him for drinking wine insofar as he relied on his certitude, albeit erroneously. This is one of the two aspects of 'evidentiary knowledge' (*ḥujjiyat al-'ilm*), and it can be termed 'the aspect of excusability' (*jānib al-mu'adhdhiriyyah*).

2. When a believer disobeys his Lord as a result of not acting according to his own belief and certitude, the Lord is justified in punishing him and holding his certitude against him. An example would be a person unequivocally certain that the drink in front of him is wine who proceeds to drink it. In this case, the Lord has the right to punish him for his disobedience, because he drank the wine despite his knowledge that wine is prohibited; he has no excuse. This is the second aspect of

evidentiary certitude, and it can be termed 'the aspect of materialization' (*jānib al-munajjiziyah*).

It is clear that evidentiary certitude, in the meaning explained above, is indispensable to all procedures for the derivation of *shar'i* rulings. For the jurist always emerges from the procedure of derivation with a given result, which is the knowledge of the practical standpoint with regard to the Sharī'ā and a definition of it based either on evidence or on a practical principle. For this result to be effective, one must admit in advance the principle of evidentiary certitude. Without such certitude, which permits the Lord to level a charge against the believer and the believer to argue before his Lord, the result of the procedure of derivation arrived at by the jurist will be null and void, for it is lacking in evidentiary certitude. It is therefore necessary that the element of evidentiary certitude be present in every procedure of derivation so that the procedure may bear fruit and the jurist produce a positive result. Evidentiary certitude is thus seen to be the most general and wide-ranging of the common elements.

Indeed, it is not merely a common element in the procedure of the derivation of religious rulings by the jurist, but also in reality a fundamental precondition for the study of the common elements themselves by the scholars. Thus, when we study the question of the authority of tradition or the authority of the apparent usage as reflected in a text, we are attempting to gain true knowledge of these issues; were knowledge and certitude not to be considered as proofs, what benefit would there be in studying the authority of tradition or of the apparent usage?

Both the jurist and the scholar of legal theory aim, by means of their investigations, to acquire knowledge. This knowledge is either of a juridical nature, i.e. defining the practical standpoint vis-a-vis the Sharī'ā, or of a theoretical nature, i.e. defining the 'common element'. Thus, without prior acknowledgement of the authority of knowledge (*ḥujjiyat al-'ilm*) and of certitude (*ḥujjiyat al-qat'*), their studies would be useless and futile.

The authority of certitude is established by the decree of reason that the Lord (glory be unto Him) has the right to be obeyed by man in whatever obligations, including commands and prohibitions, He places upon him and of which he is aware.

Thus, if one knows of a 'binding ruling' (*ḥukm ilzāmī*) from the Lord, be it of obligatoriness or prohibition, it falls under the heading of the right of obedience. Thus it is the Lord's right to be obeyed by human beings in whatever they know to be their duty. If they are negligent in that respect or fail in their duty of obedience, they deserve punishment. This is the materialization aspect (*al-munajjiziah*) regarding the authority of certitude.

On the other hand, the intellect also decrees that a person who is certain about not having a duty in a particular matter can act as he sees fit. If in such circumstances a ruling does, however, exist, it is not the Lord's right to demand obedience, nor is it justified for the Lord to punish those who disobey Him in that regard, as long as they are certain about the absence of a duty. This is the 'excusability' (*al-mu'adhdhiriyyah*) aspect in the authority of certitude.

In the same way that the intellect comprehends the authority of certitude, it also comprehends that it is not possible to remove authority from certitude, for it is concomitant with it. It is not possible even for the Lord to separate authority from certitude, for this would amount to the statement that, 'even when you are certain that you have no duty, you are still not excused,' or, 'even when you are certain about having a duty, you can still disregard it'. The intellect recognizes that such statements cannot possibly be valid. This is because neither excusability nor materialization is ever separable from certitude: hence the principle of legal theory that states that it is impossible for the Legislator to prohibit an action based in certitude.

It might be argued that in view of this precept, if a person believes erroneously that drinking wine, for example, is lawful, the Lord should not inform him of his error. The reply would be that it is possible for the Lord to make a person aware of his error and inform him that the wine is not permissible. That will remove his certitude and restore him to correct action. The aforementioned precept simply affirms the impossibility of the Lord's prohibiting an action performed on the basis of certitude while that certitude persists.

It is possible for the Lord to remove the certitude of a person who believes that drinking wine is lawful. However, as long as his certitude and his belief in permissibility persist, it is impossible for the Lord to prohibit him to act according to his certitude.

LESSON EIGHT

General Principles

The evidence that the jurist relies upon for the derivation of a *shar'i* ruling either leads to knowledge of a ruling or it does not.

In the first case, the evidence is definitive (*qaṭ'i*) and derives its legality and authority from the authority of certitude because it leads to the certitude regarding the ruling. Reason recognizes the authority of certitude, and it is incumbent on the jurist to base his deduction of a *shar'i* ruling upon it.

An example of this is the formula: 'Whenever a matter is obligatory its prerequisite is also obligatory.' This formula is considered to be definitive evidence for the necessity of ablution as a prerequisite for prayer.

In the second case the evidence is inadequate because it is not definitive. However, if the Legislator authorizes the inadequate evidence and instructs us to rely on it in the procedure of derivation, it will then become like definitive evidence, in spite of its inadequacy, and it will be imperative for the jurist to rely on it. An example of the inadequate evidence designated by the Legislator as a proof is 'the report of a trustworthy person' (*khabar al-thiqah*). Such a report does not lead to certain knowledge because of the possibility of mistakes or deviations from the norm. However, despite its inadequacy and conjectural nature, such a report has been made a proof by the Legislator and He has instructed us to accept and follow it. For this reason, it is elevated to the level of definitive evidence in the procedure of derivation.

If the Legislator does not bestow authority on inadequate evidence, it cannot be taken as a proof or relied on for derivation of a religious ruling, because it bears within it the possibility of error. Sometimes, however, we are uncertain whether or not the Legislator has authorized inadequate evidence as a proof or not, and no proof is available to affirm or to deny such authorization. In such cases it is necessary to refer to a general precept established by the scholars of the principles of jurisprudence, which states: 'No inadequate evidence counts as an authorized proof unless it is not established as such by revelational evidence.' This is what is meant by the statement we find in the science of the principles of jurisprudence that 'No conjecture is principally authorized unless it is proved by definitive evidence.' We conclude from this that the evidence fit to be relied upon in jurisprudence is either definitive evidence or inadequate evidence the legal authority of which is proven through definitive evidence.

Securing evidence, whether definitive or not, is divided into two categories:

First, *shar'i* evidence, which is everything issuing from the Legislator that points to a ruling; it consists of the Qur'ān and the Sunnah, the latter being the words, actions and tacit approvals of the Maʿsūm in (the Prophet and the Imāms (AS)).

Second, rational evidence, by which is meant propositions that reason comprehends and from which it is possible to derive a *shar'i* ruling, such as the proposition that states: 'The obligatoriness of an act necessitates the obligatoriness of its prerequisites.'

The first type in turn is subdivided into verbal *shar'i* evidence, the words of the Legislator as expressed in the Qur'ān and the Sunnah, and non-verbal *shar'i* evidence, an example being the action of a Maʿsūm or his tacit approval, i.e. his remaining silent regarding an action of another person in such a way as to indicate his acceptance of it.

With respect to both types we must know (1) the signification (*al-dalālah*) of the evidence in accordance with the apparent sense of conventional usage; (2) the authority of that signification and of its apparent sense, and whether it is necessary to rely on it; and (3) whether the evidence did in fact issue from the Legislator. We will deal with each of these issues in turn.

LESSON NINE

Signification or Indication

Since the question of the 'indication' of the verbal evidence is connected with the general linguistic system of meaning, we will precede our discussion of it with a brief study of the nature of that system and the manner of its formation.

In every language there are established relationships between a collection of words and a collection of meanings. Every word is associated with a specific meaning in a way that enables our mind, when we conceive the word, to move immediately to conceiving the meaning. This association between conception of the word and conception of the meaning, and the movement of the mind from one to the other, is what is termed 'the indication' (*al-dalālah*). Therefore, when we say, 'The word "water" indicates a specific liquid', we mean that conceptualizing the word 'water' leads to conceptualizing that specific liquid. Thus, we call the word 'the indicator' and the meaning 'the indicated'. On this basis, we understand that the relationship between the conceptualization of the word and the conceptualization of the meaning resembles, to some extent, the relationship that we observe in our daily life between fire and heat or between the rising of the sun and the appearance of light. In the same way that fire leads to heat and the rising of the sun to daylight, the conceptualization of the word leads to the conceptualization of the meaning. It is thus possible to state that the conceptualization of the word is a cause for the conceptualization of the meaning, just as fire is a cause for heat and the rising of the sun for daylight. However, the causative relationship between the conceptualization of the word and the conceptualization of the meaning plays out in the mind, whereas the causative relationship between fire and heat or the rising of the sun and daylight exists in the external world.

The basic question with regard to the connection within language between the word and the meaning is about the origin of this relationship and the way in which it is established. How did the relationship of causality between the word and the meaning originate, and in what manner did the conceptualization of the word become a cause for the conceptualization of the meaning, despite the fact that the word and the meaning are two totally different things?

Usually two views are given in the science of *uṣūl* in reply to these questions. The first is based on the belief that the relationship of the word to the meaning arises from the inherent nature of the word itself, just as the relationship of fire with heat arises from the inherent nature of fire. Thus, the word 'water' has by virtue of its nature a relationship with the specific meaning that we comprehend from it. This view insists that the meaning indicated by a word is inherent to it and is not derived from any external cause.

However, this view is unable fully to explain the situation, because if the meaning indicated by a word is inherent to it and did not originate from any external cause, and the word impels the mind towards the conceptualization of its meaning simply by its inherent nature, why is a non-Arab unable to conceptualize the meaning of the word *mā'* ('water') when he conceptualizes the word? And second, why does he need to learn the Arabic language before his mind can move to the meaning when he hears the Arabic word and tries to conceptualize it?

This suggests that the relationship formed in the mind between the conception of the word and the conception of the meaning does not originate from the inherent nature of the word, but rather from another cause, the acquisition of which demands the learning of the Arabic language. The meaning indicated by a word cannot therefore be inherent in it.

The other view rightly denies the inherency of the indicated meaning and hypothesizes that the relationships between words and their meanings in every language were established by the first person or persons who produced and spoke that language. They specified particular words for particular meanings, as a result of which words acquired a relationship with meanings and each word came to indicate its own particular meaning. That specification process practised by those first people among whom the word–meaning nexus arose may be termed 'postulation' (*waḍ'*) and its practitioner 'postulator' (*wāḍi'*); the word is the 'postulated' (*al-mawḍū'*) and the meaning indicated by it is 'that for which it was postulated' (*al-mawḍūʿ lahu*).

Even though this second view is right in its refutation of the inherency theory, it takes us only one step towards solving the basic problem. Suppose we concede that the relationship of causality is due to an action on the part of the inventor of the language, by which he specifies a meaning for every word; we must still inquire into the nature of the action performed by the inventor. For if there is no inherent relationship between word and meaning and no prior association has been established, how it is possible for the inventor of language to create a previously non-existent relationship of causality between two things? Is the sole fact of specifying a word and designating it as a cause for the conceptualization of a meaning sufficient actually to make it the cause for the conceptualization of that meaning? It is obvious that neither the inventor of a language nor any other person is capable of making the redness of the ink with which he is writing become a cause for water temperature, even if he repeats the attempt a hundred times saying, 'I specify that the redness of the ink with which I am writing to be a cause for water temperature'. So how is it possible for him to succeed in making the word a cause for the conceptualization of the meaning by mere specification in the absence of any prior relationship? This takes us back to the original problem. Therefore, to explain the relationship between the word and the meaning on the basis of an action of the inventor of the language also fails to offer an adequate solution. We must understand the contents of the procedure involved in order to grasp how the relationship of causality was established between two things not joined by any prior relationship.

The way to solve this problem is to understand that the relationship of causality established in language between word and meaning is created in accordance with a general rule of the human mind. This rule states that if two things are repeatedly conceptualized in the mind in association with each other, even if by coincidence, a relationship is established between the two so that one of the conceptualizations becomes a cause for the mind to move directly to the other.

An example of this in our day-to-day life would be that if we were living with two friends who were never apart in any aspect of their lives and whom we always found together at any given time, whenever we subsequently saw one of them alone or heard the name of only one of them, our mind would rapidly rush towards the conceptualization of the other because seeing them together repeatedly would have created a relationship in our conceptualization. That relationship would have made our conceptualization of one of them a cause for the conceptualization of the other.

Occasionally it is sufficient to associate only once the conceptualization of one of two things with the conceptualization of the other in order to establish a relationship between the two. This becomes possible when the two concepts are associated in some particularly influential circumstance. For example, if a person travels to a certain town, becomes severely afflicted there with malaria and then recovers and returns home, the association between malaria and his journey to that town will result in the formation of a relationship between the two; whenever he conceptualizes that town, his mind will immediately move to the conceptualization of malaria. Thus if we study the relationship of causality between word and meaning on this basis, the problem will be solved. For we will be able to explain the relationship by describing it as the result of an association between the conceptualization of the meaning and the conceptualization of the word, an association following on repeated joint conceptualization or an influential circumstance. However, a question remains still to be answered, namely, how does the conceptualization of the word in repeated association with a specific meaning or in some influential circumstance result in the establishment of a linguistic association between the two?

The answer is that some words are associated repeatedly with specific meanings in a spontaneous manner, as a result of which a linguistic relationship is established between them.

An example of this is the exclamation 'ow', which is naturally uttered by a person feeling pain, thereby connecting the word 'ow' with the thought of pain. As a result whenever he hears the word 'ow', his mind moves immediately to the conceptualization of pain. It is probable that prior to the existence of language, the attention of people was drawn to the spontaneous association existing between such words as 'ow' and the concept of pain, which then led to the development of different kinds of association between words and their meanings.

Some words are linked to their meanings through a consciously intended procedure with the aim of establishing a relationship of causality between them. The best examples of this are proper names that are deliberately attached to a person, for example to a newborn child, in order to create a linguistic relationship between the two, so that the name becomes an indicator of the child. This process is called 'convention', the procedure of connecting a word to a specific meaning, the result of which is conceptualization of the meaning in the mind whenever the word is conceptualized.

The process of convention could be compared to a case in which a person asks for an optician to be recommended to him and is given the name of Jābir. In order to remember the name he will attempt to relate it to something more familiar to him. For example, if he has read a captivating book and the name of the author was Jābir, he will condition his mind to recall the name of the author whenever he wants to remember the name of the optician. In this specific manner, a connection is made between the two words and the person is reminded of the optician's name whenever he imagines that book.

This method of creating a connection between two things does not differ in essence from the act of convention as a means to bring about a linguistic relationship between a word and its meaning. We thus realize that as result of convention, the meaning for which the word is postulated comes spontaneously to mind whenever the word is mentioned because of the relationship previously established between the two.

It is thus possible to suggest that the spontaneous occurrence to the mind of a given meaning upon hearing a given word is a proof that the word in question was postulated for the meaning in question. In other words, spontaneous occurrence is a sign suggesting that the meaning so occurring is also the meaning for which the word was postulated, for effect reveals cause. Spontaneously occurring meaning therefore serves to determine the true meaning of a word.

Usage

Once a word is postulated for a given meaning, the conceptualization of the word becomes a cause for the conceptualization of the meaning. You then use this linguistic relationship to express the same meaning to another person and to bring him to conceptualize it in his mind. You may utter the word that has become a cause for the conceptualization of the meaning, and when your friend hears it his mind moves immediately to the meaning because of the causative relationship existing between word and meaning. This use of the word in order to convey its meaning to the mind of the hearer is called usage.

To put it differently, the usage of a word is the production of a word by one person in order to prepare the mind of another for the reception of its meaning. The word employed in this way is known as 'the used' (*al-musta'mal*), and the meaning in which it is employed is called 'that for which it is used' (*al-musta'mal fihi*). The intention of the one employing the word to convey its meaning to the mind of the listener is termed 'the intention of usage' (*irāda isti'maliyyah*).

Every form of usage will require the user to conceptualize the word and its meaning. However, the conceptualization of the word is usually an instrumental awareness (*liḥāẕ 'ālī*) while that of the meaning is an autonomous awareness (*liḥāẕ istiqlālī*). The two resemble respectively a mirror and the image it reflects. You look at a mirror in order to view the reflection while ignoring the existence of the mirror itself. Similarly, you are aware of the word only to the degree that it serves as a mirror for the meaning; you ignore the existence of the word itself, since your gaze is focused on the meaning.

It might be objected that it cannot be possible to be aware of a word and to ignore it at the same time, for this would be an obvious contradiction. The answer is that instrumental awareness of the word is equivalent to its dissolution in the meaning; the word is dissolved in the meaning and is the object of awareness only through awareness of the meaning. Awareness of a thing as having been dissolved in another is compatible with unawareness of it in its own right.

Based on this, a group of scholars such as the author of *al-Kifāyah* have asserted the impossibility of using a single word in two different meanings because such an operation would require the dissolution of the same word in two different meanings at one and the same time, which is logically inconceivable.

It might be argued that you can unite two different meanings and form a compound of them that contains both of them, and then regard the word as dissolved in that compounded meaning. Although this is possible, you would still be using a word for one meaning, not for two meanings.

*Literal (*al-Ḥaqīqa*) and Metaphorical (*al-Majāz*) Meaning*

The usage of a word falls into the categories of literal and metaphorical. The literal usage of the word consists of its use with the meaning for which it was specified and with which it has established a linguistic connection by means of convention. The meaning for which the word was postulated is therefore termed 'literal meaning.'

Metaphorical usage entails the use of a word in a meaning for which it was not postulated but which resembles the postulated meaning for one reason or another. An example of this would be to use the word 'sea' to indicate a scholar profusely endowed with knowledge because of his resemblance to the sea with respect to abundance and expanse. The term 'metaphorical meaning' is therefore used to describe a meaning bearing some resemblance to the literal meaning for which the word was postulated.

The relationship and the connection of the word with its metaphorical meaning is a

secondary one, deriving from the primary linguistic connection the word has with its literal meaning. This is because the relationship between the word and its metaphorical meaning is a consequence of the similarity existing between it and the meaning for which the word was postulated.

The literal usage of the word leads directly to the attainment of its objective, which is to impel the mind of the listener to conceptualization of the meaning, without the need to fulfil any conditions. This is guaranteed in any language by the causative relationship existing between meanings and their postulated words.

By contrast, metaphorical usage does not impel the listener's mind immediately to conceptualize the metaphorical meaning, for no linguistic connection or causative relationship exists between, for example, the word 'sea' and the meaning 'scholar'. To attain his goal, the user will therefore need to supply a contextual clarifier in order to make his purpose plain. Thus, if one says 'a sea of knowledge', for example, the word 'knowledge' will serve as a context indicating metaphorical usage of the word 'sea'.

It is often said therefore that a metaphorical usage needs a context whereas a literal usage does not. We distinguish the literal from the metaphorical meaning of a word through the process of spontaneous occurrence of a meaning to the mind immediately on hearing the word. For, as already stated, such spontaneous occurrence reveals to us the meaning for which the word was postulated.

Change of a Metaphorical Meaning to a Literal Meaning

The scholars of legal theory have rightly noted that sometimes the metaphorical usage of a word – although initially it is in need of a contextual clarifier – may be repeated with such frequency that it results in the establishment of a new bond between the word and its metaphorical meaning, to the extent that the word becomes postulated for the metaphorical meaning. The metaphorical meaning of the word thus comes to resemble its literal meaning and subsequently will no longer need a contextual clarifier to be conveyed by means of the word in question. Such a process of postulation is termed 'self-specifying postulation' (*al-waḍ' al-ta'āyunī*), whereas the process of a postulator stipulating a specific word for a meaning is called 'specifying postulation' (*al-waḍ' al-ta'yīnī*).

This phenomenon can easily be explained in light of our description of the nature of postulation and the linguistic bond. The linguistic relationship between a word and its meaning results from repeated concomitance of the word with its meaning or its conjunction with the meaning in influential circumstances. Thus if a word is frequently used in its metaphorical meaning, a relationship is created in the mind of the listener between the conceptualization of the word and that of the metaphorical meaning by virtue of their union; this in turn leads to the establishment of a linguistic bond between the two.

LESSON ELEVEN

Dividing Meanings into Nominal (*Ismī*) and Particular (*Ḥarfī*)

As you will have learnt when studying syntax, words may be nouns, verbs or particles.

Nouns indicate their meanings by themselves, whether uttered in isolation or in the context of a statement. By contrast, particles do not yield any meaning except in the context of a statement. In other words, what is denoted by a particle is always some type of connection between nominal meanings.

For example, in our statement 'the fire in the stove is burning', the particle 'in' signifies a specific connection between the two nominal concepts of 'fire' and 'stove'.

The evidence that the signification of particles is a bond existing between nominal meanings is twofold:

1. The meaning of a particle is not evident if the particle is removed from the sentence, precisely because the purpose of the particle is to signify the relationship existing between the nominal meanings. Once the particle is considered on its own, there is no room for supposing a connection.

2. Self-evidently, a sentence is constructed from parts whose meaning is interconnected. There is also no doubt that this interconnected meaning consists of elements that supply the connections and others that are connected to each other. It is not possible to have different parts connected with each other without something to indicate those connections, for otherwise the meanings of words within a statement would come to the mind in a scattered form. However, the noun

cannot serve the purpose of signifying a connection, for otherwise it would be incomprehensible except in the context of a sentence, for connection cannot be conceived in the absence of meanings that require interconnection. It is clear therefore that it is the particle that signifies the connections between the nominal meanings.

Different particles signify different types of connection, and since every connection constitutes a relationship between two termini, it is proper to say that the meanings conveyed by particles are connective and relational meanings whereas the nominal meanings are independent meanings. We therefore term 'particle' whatever conveys a connective and relational meaning and 'noun' whatever conveys an independent meaning.

As for a verb, it is a compound of substance and shape. By 'substance' we mean the original form from which it is derived and by 'structure' the paradigmatic pattern into which the substance is inserted.

The substance of a verb is no different from a noun. Thus the verb *tashta'il* ('is burning') has as its substance *al-ishti'āl* ('burning', as a gerund), which has a nominal meaning. However, a verb is not equivalent to the meaning indicated by its substance; it exceeds it, as can be seen from the impermissibility of substituting *ishti'āl* for *tashta'il*. It is by virtue of its structue that the verb goes beyond the meaning indicated by its substance. The structure of the verb is postulated for a specific meaning separate from independent nominal meaning. Otherwise it would be possible to replace a verb with two nouns, one signifying its structural meaning and the other indicating its substantial meaning. This we know to be impossible, and we therefore conclude that the meaning that is indicated by the structure of a verb is a relational and connective meaning. It is for this reason that a structural signification cannot be replaced by an equivalent nominal meaning. The connection implied by the structure of the verb is a connection established between the signification of the substance and another signification, like that of a subject. For example, in the phrase 'the fire is burning', the structure of the verb implies a connection between burning and the fire.

In short, a verb may be regarded as a compound of noun and particle, the substance of the verb being a noun and its structure a particle. Thus, it is correct to state that language is constructed only of two elements, nouns and particles.

Sentence Structure

Verbs, then, have a structure signifying a particular meaning akin to that of a particle, for it indicates connection among nominal meanings. The same is the case with sentences. By 'sentence' we mean two or more words connected together. Thus in the sentence, 'Alī is an Imām ' we comprehend nominal meanings for both the words 'Alī' and 'Imām ', and additionally we understand a specific bond to exist between these two words that is not signified by either of them. This connection between the two words is indicated by the specific structure of the sentence, so that the sentence comes to bear a meaning akin to that of a particle.

We may summarize the foregoing by concluding that language consists of two categories of meaning: nominal meanings, including both nouns and the substances of verbs and connective meanings, including particles, verb structures and sentence structures.

Complete and Incomplete Sentences

On observing sentences we find that some of them signify a complete meaning that it is possible for the speaker to convey by means of them and for the listener to verify or falsify, while others are incomplete and do not yield any information; they are comparable in their signification to a single word. An example would be to say, 'al-Mufīd the scholar', which would amount to the same as saying simply, 'al-Mufīd ', for in both cases the listener is left waiting for the statement to be completed. This is in contrast to the statement, 'al-Mufīd is a scholar', which signifies a complete meaning.

The point of difference between a complete and an incomplete sentence is in the type of connection indicated by the structure of the sentence. The incomplete sentence signifies a fusional relationship between the nominal meanings insofar as it fuses the attribute and the noun it qualifies into a single meaning having the effect of a single word. The complete sentence, by contrast, signifies a non-fusional relationship between its parts leaving them distinct from each other, so that the listener hears two distinct parts of a statement specifically connected with each other, as is the case with a subject and its predicate. A single sentence may sometimes contain both fusional and non-fusional relationships. An example would be the sentence, 'al-Mufīd the scholar is a lecturer', in which there is a fusional relationship in the subject between the attribute and the noun it qualifies and a non-fusional relationship between the subject and the predicate. The completeness of the sentence results from the non-fusional relationship between the subject and the predicate.

If we examine incomplete sentences containing particles such as 'from' and 'to', we find that they too indicate incomplete relationships and connections that it would not be proper to utter on their own. Thus, just as it would not be proper to say, 'al-Mufīd the scholar' and then to remain silent, so too it would be incorrect to say, 'the journey from Basrah'. This shows that particles used in an incomplete sentence structure signify fusional relationships, in contrast to the complete sentence, whether nominal or verbal, that signifies a non-fusional connection.

Linguistic Signification and Confirmational Signification

As stated earlier, a word signifies meaning in that conceptualization of the word itself leads to the conceptualization of the meaning; in this process, the word is termed the 'indicator' (signifier) and the meaning the 'indicated' (signified). This is linguistic signification, created by the postulation of a word for a meaning; postulation brings about a causative relationship between the conceptualization of the word and the conceptualization of the meaning. The meaning signified in this way is termed the linguistic meaning of the word.

The linguistic signification of a word cannot be separated from it irrespective of how the word is produced. Let us take as an example the statement, 'truth prevails'; as soon as we hear this sentence our minds immediately conceive its linguistic meaning, whether it emanates from a conscious speaker, from someone talking in his sleep or even from two stones being knocked together. We immediately conceive the meanings of the words, 'truth' and 'prevails', and the non-fusional complete relationship between the two for which the structure of the sentence is postulated. It is on account of this that such an indication is termed 'conceptual signification'.

If, however, we compare the possibilities mentioned above with regard to the utterance of the statement, we find that when the sentence is uttered by an unconscious speaker or results from two stones being knocked together, it conveys only its linguistic signification, creating in our minds conceptions of 'truth' and 'prevail' existing in a complete relationship with each other. Now, if uttered by a conscious speaker, the signification of the statement transcends the level of mere concepts and attains that of acknowledgement, for we deduce certain things concerning what the speaker has in his mind when uttering it. When a conscious speaker utters a statement, certainly he intends us to conceive its linguistic meanings, this being termed his 'intention of usage', but his motive is not simply to create abstract concepts in our minds. He also has a fundamental purpose of his own, which in the example given above is to affirm the relationship between the subject and the predicate. This fundamental purpose or motive on the part of the speaker is termed the 'serious intention'.

To describe both these intentions, i.e. the 'intention of usage' and 'serious intention', we use the term 'confirmational signification', for taken together they disclose to us the intention of the speaker and require us to confirm it, not simply to conceive it. Thus we see that a complete statement in addition to its conceptual signification has two confirmational significations:

1. The intention of usage, because we know that when a speaker utters a statement he intends us to conceptualize the meanings of the words it contains.

2. The serious intention, which is the primary objective for the sake of which the speaker intended us to conceptualize his words.

Sometimes a statement may not have the second of these two, as happens when a statement is made in jest. It will then have only the first confirmational signification, i.e. the intention of usage, without the motive of affirming the relationship of the predicate with its subject. The confirmational signification in not linguistic, in the sense that it is not an expression of the relationship arrived at by virtue of the process of postulation between the word and its confirmational signification. This is because postulation brings about a connection between conceptualization of the word and conceptualization of its meaning, not between conceptualization of the word and its confirmational signification.

This latter can be deduced only from the state of the speaker. Thus if someone says, while conscious, awake and serious, 'truth prevails', his state will indicate to us that he did not say it in jest or unintentionally, but with a conscious and specific intention. When we hear the statement, 'truth prevails', we first conceptualize the linguistic meanings of its subject and predicate by virtue of the causative linguistic bond formed by postulation between the word and its meaning. We next discover the intention of conscious usage in the mind of the speaker from his apparent state. The first represents the conceptual signification and the meaning we conceptualize through it is known as the conceptually or linguistically signified meaning of the word and the statement. The second, i.e. the discovery of the user's intention, represents the confirmational signification; that which is signified is termed the confirmationally signified and is deduced from the state of the speaker.

We thus discover two sources for signification:

1. Language and its postulations, the source for the conceptual indication.

2. The state of the speaker, the source for confirmational indication, i.e. the signification of the word in its confirmational meaning. A statement can only disclose the intention of the speaker if he utters it while awake, aware and serious, because this state alone is the source for confirmational signification. If a speaker utters a statement while asleep or by way of jest, no confirmtional indication attaches to his statement.

Declarative and Exclamatory Sentences

The statements are normally divided into declarative and exclamatory. The difference between the two is obvious. If, for example, we heard the statement, 'I sold the book yesterday for a dinar', we should see clearly that it differs substantially from the statement, 'I am selling you the book for a dinar', for in the latter case a transaction is being offered at the present time.

Despite the fact that both of the statements comprise complete non-fusional relationships between the transaction and the seller, there is a difference in our understanding of the two statements and in our conceptualization of the type of connections contained in them. Thus when the speaker says, 'I sold the book for a dinar', informing us of an event that has already taken place, we conceive a relationship between the seller and the transaction as a completed event over which he no longer has any control; all he can do is inform others of it. However, if the statement is, 'I am selling you the book for a dinar', the relationship between the seller and the transaction is not conceived of as a completed event but as a relationship the statement is intended to actualize.

In short, the declarative statement is postulated to convey a completed relationship that has already taken place, while the exclamatory statement is postulated to indicate a complete relationship, the occurrence of which is intended at the time of its utterance. Some scholars, however, like the author of *al-Kifāyah*, are of the opinion that the relationship in the statement 'I sell' in both its declarative and exclamatory forms is the same and that there is no difference between them at the level of postulation and conceptual signification. The only difference is at the level of the confirmational signification. This is because when speaking to a buyer, a seller will use the statement 'I sell' to express his intention of transferring ownership and establishing a contract, while speaking to others he will simply be informing them of what has transpired. The difference lies in the confirmational signification, not the conceptual signification.

It is obvious that such an assertion can be valid only in those cases where a common expression is used for both the declaratory and exclamatory instances, as is the case with the statement 'I sell'. It does not apply to statements that are specific in expressing either a declaratory and or an exclamatory purpose. An example of this is the imperative form, which is an exclamatory statement; it cannot be used to inform others about the occurrence of an event, but only to signify the demand for its occurrence. It is not possible in such cases to say, for example, that the conceptual signification of the imperative form 'don't do it' is the same as the conceptual signification of a declaratory sentence, and that the difference in indication is only perceivable at the level of confirmational signification. The proof of this is that we are conscious of the difference between the two types of statement even if they are isolated from their confirmational significations, as is the case when we hear them from a speaker who has no awareness of what he is saying.

What Indications Are Discussed in the Principles of Jurisprudence?

For the purposes of *uṣūl al-fiqh*, it is possible to divide linguistic elements into the specific elements and the common elements in the procedure of derivation.

The common elements are all the linguistic forms that may appropriately be included in any evidence (*dalīl*) regardless of the subject to which that evidence relates, an example being the imperative form of the verb, which can be used in relation to any subject.

The specific elements in the procedure of derivation are the linguistic forms that can be included only in a single evidence dealing with a specific subject, and cannot be used to derive a ruling in any other field. An example of this is the word '*al-iḥsan*' ('to do good to others'), since it cannot be included in evidence for rulings other than those related to doing good. Conversely, an evidence for a ruling connected with prayers, for example, will have no relevance to a ruling connected with doing good. The word *al-iḥsan* is a specific element in the derivation process.

The science of the principles of jurisprudence studies those linguistic forms that are considered to be common elements in the procedure of derivation. Thus it deals with such questions as the indication of the imperative form and whether it implies obligation or recommendation, not with the meanings and signification of individual words such as *al-iḥsan*.

Among the linguistic forms that can be considered as a part of the common linguistic elements are the conditional particles because of their relevance to the derivation of a ruling from its evidence. For example, from the text that specifies, 'when the sun moves from its zenith the prayers become obligatory', we deduce, because of the conditional particle, that the obligation of prayer is connected to the movement of the sun from its zenith. Similarly, we deduce from the text, 'fasting becomes obligatory when the crescent of the month of Ramadan appears', that the obligation of the fast is connected to the appearance of the crescent. The discipline of the principles of jurisprudence therefore studies the conditional particles as common elements in the procedure of derivation, and it explores the various kinds of connection they imply and their consequences for the derivation of religious rulings.

The same is the case with the form of the plural attached to the definite article (*al-*), since such a particle will be relevant to the textual evidence for any subject.

We will now discuss some examples of these common elements as studied by the scholars of legal theory.

*The Imperative Form (*Ṣīghat al-Amr*)*

The imperative form is exemplified by verbs such as *idhhab* ('go'), *ṣalli* ('pray'), *ṣūm* ('fast') and *jāhid* ('fight'). It is generally accepted by the legists that these forms linguistically signify obligation. However, we may well ask whether the scholars mean that the imperative form has precisely the same signification as obligation (*al-wujūb*) so that the two are synonymous. We feel instinctively that there is a difference between the two, for if there were not, it would be proper to use one in place of the other, which is clearly not possible. We conclude, therefore, that the imperative does imply a meaning different from that conveyed by the word obligation. It is difficult to understand the assertion, often repeated by the scholars, of the legal theory that the imperative form implies obligation.

However, in order to comprehend what is at issue, let us analyse the ways in which the imperative may signify obligation. If we examine the imperative verb, we find that the relationship between the substance of the verb and its subject is one the realization of the which is desired by impelling the one addressed to create it. Think of a hunter sending his dog off in pursuit of its prey. The image contemplated by the hunter of his dog as he sends it off in pursuit of its prey is exactly the same as that signified by the imperative verb. For this reason what is signified by the imperative form is known in the science of the principles of jurisprudence as the 'relationship of sending or impelling' (*al-nisbah al-irsāliyyah*).

Sometimes the hunter will send his dog after the prey because of urgent longing and intense desire for the prey, whereas at other times he will do so with a less intense wish and inclination. The same is the case with the relationship of sending or impelling contained within the form of the imperative verb. We sometimes conceive of that relationship as the outcome of an intense desire and an urgent longing, and at other times as resulting from weaker desire and less insistent longing.

We are now in a position to understand what the legists mean when they assert that 'the imperative form implies obligation'. It is that the imperative form is postulated for a 'relationship of sending or impelling' resulting from intense desire and urgent longing. This is why the meanings of compulsion and obligation are incorporated in our image when we conceptualize the linguistic meaning of the imperative form as we hear it, although it is not synonymous with the word 'obligation'. The inclusion of the concepts of compulsion and obligation in the meaning of the imperative form does not mean that it cannot also be used to signify recommendation. In fact, it is used just as frequently to mean recommendation as to imply obligation. The only difference is that its usage in cases of obligation is a literal usage, that being usage in the meaning for which it is postulated. Usage of the imperative in cases of recommendation is metaphorical, for it is based on the resemblance existing between obligation and recommendation.

The proof that the imperative form is postulated to mean obligation, in the sense mentioned above, is spontaneous occurrence of that meaning in the mind of the listener as soon as he hears an imperative being uttered. This is confirmed by the fact that in conventional dealings a person who is ordered to do something by an imperative cannot claim as excuse for not discharging his duty uncertainty whether the imperative implied obligation or recommendation. The meaning spontaneously occurring to the mind of the listener is obligation, which is therefore the true as well as the literal meaning.

*The Prohibitive Form (*Ṣīghat al-Nahy*)*

An example of the prohibitive form is *lā tadhhab* ('don't go'). It is established in the principles of jurisprudence that the prohibitive form signifies prohibition (*al-ḥurmah*). In order to understand this fully, we must study the prohibitive form just as we studied the imperative form, with the difference that while the imperative conveys demand and impulsion, the prohibitive signifies restraint and prevention. The form of the prohibitive signifies a preventive or restraining relationship between the substance of the verb and its subject. On hearing the statement *idhhab* ('go') we conceive a relationship between the act of going and the one who is addressed by the command, and understand that the speaker is impelling the addressee to undertake the action in question, like a hunter sending his dog in pursuit of the prey. When we hear the statement *lā tadhhab* ('don't go'), we again conceive of a relationship between the act of going and the one addressed by the command, but picture the speaker as preventing the addressee from undertaking it; it is as if the hunter were restraining his dog from pursuing the prey. We therefore term this the preventive or restraining relationship (*al-nisbah al-imsākiyyah*). The meaning of prohibition (*al-ḥurmah*) is incorporated in the signification of the prohibitive form, just as the meaning of obligation is part of what the imperative form signifies. Let us again refer to the example of the hunter. We find that the hunter's prevention of his dog from chasing the prey may at times be a result of his intense dislike for such an act, whereas at other times it may be due to a less severe dislike. This is exactly what we find in the preventive relationship contained within the prohibitive form. For we can conceive the preventive relationship coming about at times as a result of intense dislike for the act in question and at other times from dislike of a weaker degree.

We understand from the assertion, 'the prohibitive form implies prohibition', that the form of the prohibitive is postulated for a preventive relationship arising from intense dislike, which is what we call prohibition. Thus, the meaning of prohibition is incorporated in our linguistic concept of the prohibitive form. The proof that the form of the prohibitive is postulated for prohibition is, once again, the meaning that spontaneously occurs to the mind of the listener as soon as he hears the form.

The prohibitive form is also used to convey reprehensibility (*al-karāhah*), because of the resemblance between prohibition and reprehensibility. This usage is considered to be metaphorical.

LESSON THIRTEEN

Absoluteness (*al-Iṭlāq*)

If a person wishes to order his son to respect his Muslim neighbours, he would not think it enough to tell him, 'respect the neighbours'; instead he would say, 'respect the Muslim neighbours'. If, however, he wants his son to respect neighbours irrespective of their religious beliefs and says, 'respect the neighbours', using the word 'neighbours' in an absolute and unqualified sense, his order will not be conceived of as restricted to Muslim neighbours, for it will also include the non-Muslim neighbours. This comprehensiveness is deduced from the usage of the word 'neighbour' without any qualification. Such a usage of the word is called 'absoluteness' (*al-iṭlāq*) and the word itself is termed 'absolute' (*muṭlaq*).

We can therefore assume that the freedom of a word from verbal qualification in a statement indicates comprehensiveness of the ruling. An example of this from a religiously binding text is the saying of the Almighty, 'Allah has allowed selling'. The word 'selling' (*al-bay'*) occurs here without any qualification and therefore signifies the comprehensive permissibility of all forms of selling. It might be asked how the use of a word without qualification comes to signify the comprehensiveness of a ruling. A full answer to this question lies beyond the scope of this study. In brief, however, it may be said that when the speaker has the intention to express himself, it may be inferred from his outer state that he is expressing the entirety of his intention. Thus if he says, 'respect the neighbours', while intending specifically Muslim neighbours, he will see his statement to be inadequate and will therefore add something signifying Islam. If no such qualification is made, we deduce that restriction is not a part of the speaker's intention. For if the qualification of Islam were a part of his intention but he failed to mention it, this would be contrary to the apparent state that requires him to express the entirety of his intention by means of his speech. If a speaker refrains from qualifying his speech, we therefore deduce that it is absolute in nature. The absence of qualification in a statement is termed the 'rational consort' (*qarīnat al-ḥikmah*).

*The Particles of Generality (*Adawāt al-'Umūm*)*

These are particles such as *kull* ('every') as in the statement, 'respect every just man'. When a person who commands wishes to indicate the inclusiveness and comprehensiveness of his command, he can do so by relying on the absoluteness of the word and using it without any qualification, as in the example, '*akrim al-jār*' ('respect the neighbour'). At times, however, he might wish to emphasize his intention of inclusiveness and comprehensiveness, which can be accomplished by the use of certain specific particles. The form of the command in our example could thus be amended to read, '*akrim kulla jār*' ('respect every neighbour'), from which the listener would deduce a greater emphasis on comprehensiveness and inclusiveness. Particles such as *kull* are therefore termed the 'particles of generality', for this is what they are postulated to signify. A word preceded by one of these particles is called 'general' (*'āmm*) and is designated as 'governed by the particle', insofar as the particle has endowed it with generality of meaning.

Generality can therefore be indicated in two ways:

Negatively, by simply refraining from qualifying the word, thereby using it in an absolute sense.

Affirmatively, by using the particles of generality such as *kull* ('every'), *jami'* ('all') or *kāffah* ('entirety').

The scholars of jurisprudence differ among themselves on the meaning of the plural form when combined with the definite article '*al*', as in *al-fuqahā'* ('the jurists') and *al-'uqūd* ('the transactions'). Some are of the opinion that such a form in itself is just as much a particle of generality as is the word *kull*. Thus if a speaker intended to establish a command for every individual covered by the word *fuqahā'* ('jurists') by an affirmative method, it would be enough for him to precede it with the definite article '*al*', making it a definite plural. He might then say, '*iḥtarim al-fuqahā'*' ('respect the jurists') or *awfū bi al-'uqūd* ('perform the transactions').

Others deny that the form of the definite plural is one of the particles of generality. We deduce generality and inclusiveness from a negative factor, i.e. the absence of any qualification of the word and its use in an absolute and unrestricted sense, as in statements such as '*iḥtarim al-fuqaha*'', not from an affirmative factor, i.e. from placing the definite article before the plural. Thus there is no difference between the statements, '*akrim al-faqīh*' ('honour the jurist') and '*akrim al-fuqahā*'' ('honour the jurists'), for in both cases we deduce generality from the absoluteness of the word, whether it be singular or plural.

*The Conditional Particles (*Adāt al-Sharṭ*)*

These are particles such as *idhā* ('when') as in the statement, '*idha ẓallat al-shams fa-ṣallī*' ('when the sun declines from its zenith, perform the prayer') or '*idha aḥramta li al-ḥajj fa lā tataṭayyab*' ('when you consecrate yourself for the *ḥajj*, abstain from applying fragrance'). A clause governed by a conditional particle is known as a 'conditional statement' and its linguistic function differs from that of non-conditional clauses. Non-conditional clauses consist of a linkage of one word with another, such as the subject with the predicate in a predicative statement. Conditional sentences, by contrast, consist of a linkage between two clauses, i.e. the conditional clause and the apodysis. Taken in isolation from each other, both clauses become incomplete; the conditional sentence is complete only when they are joined to each other.

On examining the two examples given above, we see that the condition in the first example is 'decline of the sun from its zenith' and, in the second, 'consecrating for the *ḥajj*', and that which is made conditional is respectively 'attend to the prayer' and 'abstain from the application of fragrance'.

We have learnt previously that the imperative form signifies obligation while the prohibitive form signifies prohibition. *Ṣalli* would indicate therefore the obligation of prayer and *lā tataṭayyab* the prohibition of using fragrance. In both cases, the ruling – obligation or prohibition – is made conditional. Whether a ruling is conditional on the decline of the sun or a state of consecration depends on the fact that it is made contingent upon it; plainly enough, that which is made conditional on something else terminates with the termination of the condition.

The conditional particle signifies therefore the absence of a ruling in the absence of the relevant condition, since this is the meaning of making a ruling contingent on a given factor. The sentence 'when the sun moves from its zenith, attend to the prayer' indicates the absence of any obligation to perform the prayer before the sun declines from its zenith.

Similarly, the sentence 'when you consecrate yourself for the *ḥajj*, abstain from the application of fragrance' indicates the permissibility of its application before the state of consecration. A conditional statement has therefore two forms of indication: affirmative, indicating the consequence that follows on the existence of the condition, and negative, indicating cessation of the consequence when the condition ceases to exist. The affirmative indication is called *manṭūq*, the spoken or explicit meaning of the statement, and its negative indication is called *mafhūm*, the implied meaning.

Every statement with a negative indication is said in jurisprudence to have an implied meaning. Some scholars have formulated a general principle for such negative indications by saying, 'every linguistic particle indicating the restriction and limitation of a ruling has a negative indication'. For the particle signifies the cessation of the ruling beyond the limitations that are stipulated for it. The conditional particle is considered to be an instance of this principle, since it makes the ruling contingent on a condition. Among other instances of this principle are *adāt al-ghāyah* ('particles of duration'), as in '*ṣūm ḥatta taghīb al-shams*' ('fast until the sun disappears'). Here the word *ṣūm* ('fast') is an imperative signifying obligation but it is given a fixed duration by the word *ḥatta* ('until'), a particle of duration. This particle restricts the obligation of fasting and signifies its cessation after the sun has set. This is a negative or implied indication. The negative indication of a conditional sentence is called *mafhūm al-sharṭ* ('the implied meaning of the condition'), while the negative indication of a particle of duration is called *mafhūm al-ghāyah* ('the implied meaning of the particle of duration').

However, in such statements as, 'be generous to the poor who are virtuous', the adjective 'virtuous' does not indicate that generosity to the poor who are sinful is unnecessary. This is because the existence of 'virtue' in the poor is not a limiting qualification on which the ruling is made conditional; it is simply an adjective describing the poor, and as long as the qualification does not relate directly to the ruling, a statement of this kind will not be regarded as having an implied meaning. For this reason it is said that in general an adjective has no implied meaning, as in the example we have given.

The Authority of Apparent Meaning and State (*Ḥujjiyyat al-Ẓuhūr*)

When considering a legal evidence (*dalīl shar'ī*) it is not enough to interpret it at the level of its linguistic conceptual signification. It is also necessary to understand it in the context of its confirmational signification in order to deduce from it the intention of the Lawgiver. We often find a word to have several linguistic and conventional significations and in order to understand what the speaker intended by uttering it we have recourse to two forms of apparence.

First, the apparent meaning of the word at the level of conceptual signification, i.e. the meaning that most immediately suggests itself when one hears the word, as distinct from all other meanings within the realm of linguistic possibility.

Second, the apparent state of the speaker suggesting that his intention and choice of meaning from the word is in accordance with the meaning the word has at the level of its conceptual signification. To put it differently, he intends to convey the most immediate of the word's linguistically possible meanings. This is known as 'the appearance of congruity between the established meaning of a word and that which the speaker wishes to affirm'.

It is an established principle of jurisprudence that the apparent state of the speaker indicating his use of the word in its most immediate sense is authoritative. By this principle is meant that the apparent state is to be taken as a basis for the interpretation of the textual evidence. We consistently assume that the speaker intends to use the word in its most immediate linguistic meaning, basing ourselves on his apparent state. This authority of the two forms of appearance is termed *aṣālat al-ẓuhūr* ('the primacy of appearance'), since it assumes them to be the essential principle in the interpretation of the textual evidence.

It can now be appreciated why in the foregoing discussions great emphasis was placed on determining the linguistic signification of a word and its apparent meaning in the general framework of the language, even though what is important in the interpretation of verbal evidence is the meaning intended by the user, not necessarily the word's most immediate lexical meaning. For the principle of the primacy of appearance shows us that a very strong connection exists between discovering the intention of the speaker and determining the most immediate lexical meaning of the word. This principle suggests that the meaning of the word intended by the speaker is in fact identical to its most immediate – i.e. apparent – lexical meaning. In order to understand the intention of the speaker we have to know first the most immediate lexical meaning of the word, and then to ascertain that it is indeed the meaning intended by the speaker.

The argument for the primacy of appearance is based on two premises:

1. that the normative conduct of the Companions of the Prophet (SAWA) and those of the Imāms was based on the apparent meaning of the Book and the Sunnah, which is indeed confirmed by the historical record of their practice;

2. that they so acted in the sight and hearing of the Prophet (SAWA) and the Imāms (AS), who did not in any way attempt to dissuade them, this demonstrating that their method was correct.

It follows from these two premises that the Legislator approves the disposition to act in accordance with apparent meaning, which establishes in turn the authority of apparent meaning and state.

Application of This Authority to Verbal Evidences

We will now examine three instances of the application of this principle.

First, let us take a case where a word contained in the verbal evidence has only one meaning and cannot signify any other, lexically or in terms of conventional usage. The general principle in such a case is to assume the word to signify that particular meaning and to conclude that the speaker intended to convey that very meaning. This is because the speaker always intends to convey a meaning of the word that is lexically assigned to it.

The evidence containing such a word will be considered to be explicit in its meaning and categorical.

In a different case, where a word has several lexical meanings all legitimately assigned to it, it will not be possible to specify the meaning intended by the speaker on the basis of the authority of apparent meaning, for lexically there is no one particular meaning closer to the word than others, making possible the application of the principle we are discussing. The evidence in which the word is used will then be considered summary (*mujmal*) in nature.

Finally, let us take the case where a word has several meanings but one is lexically closer to it than the others. The word 'sea' has the true or literal meaning of a body of water and the metaphorical meaning of 'a sea of knowledge'. Thus if someone were to tell someone else, 'go to the sea every day', and we wanted to know which of the two meanings is intended, we would first consider the context (*siyāq*) in which the word has been used. What we mean by 'context' is all the indicators surrounding the word we want to understand. Those indicators may be verbal, i.e. they may be other words, which together with the word whose meaning we want to understand form a single connected statement; or they may be circumstantial, including all the situations and circumstances that surround the speech and bear on its subject. If in all the other words appearing in the context we find nothing suggesting a meaning contrary to the apparent meaning of the word 'sea', we have no choice but to interpret the word 'sea' in terms of its most immediate lexical meaning, in accordance with the principle of the authority of apparent meaning.

On the other hand, we may find in other parts of the statement indications that do not correspond to the apparent meaning of the word 'sea'. An example of this occurs when we are told, 'go to the sea every day and attentively listen to him/it talking'. It is obvious that listening to the discourse of the sea does not accord with the most immediate lexical meaning of the word 'sea'. It corresponds instead to a scholar resembling a sea with respect to the depth of his learning. We therefore ask ourselves whether the speaker meant by 'sea' a sea of knowledge, and instructed us to listen attentively to him talking, or else a sea of water, so that what the speaker must have meant by 'talking' was not speech in its true sense, but the sound of the waves.

We are thus caught between the apparent meaning of the sea on the one hand and the apparent meaning of talking on the other, and are uncertain whether we should go to the sea and listen to the sound of its waves, as suggested by the word 'sea', or go to a learned scholar and listen to him talking, as suggested by the word 'talking'.

In such a state, we have to consider the context as a whole and to see which of the possibilities is closer to the statement according to the general functioning of the language. If such a statement were uttered to a person who knows the language and comprehends it properly would he spontaneously conceive of the first notion or the second? If we then realize that one of the two possibilities is contextually more accurate – let us suppose that it is the second option – the context as a whole must be taken as suggestive of it and the statement as a whole must be interpreted accordingly.

The word 'talking' in the example just given functions as a contextual element, because it gives the context its complete form, nullifying the apparent meaning of the word 'sea.' If, however, both possibilities pertained equally to the context of the statement, the statement would be considered ambiguous without any apparent meaning, and no possibility would exist for the application of the principle with which we are concerned.

Attached and Detached Contextual Elements

The word 'talking' serves as an 'attached contextual element' in our example because it is attached to the word 'sea', thereby nullifying the separate force of that word and establishing a single context for both. A word the separate force of which is nullified by a contextual element is termed 'contextualized' (*dhū al-qarīnah*).

Another example of an attached contextual element is provided by 'an exception from the general rule' (*al-istithnā' min al-'āmm*), as would be the case with the instruction, 'be generous to all the poor except the sinful among them'. Here the word 'all' conveys the apparent lexical meaning of generality, with which the mention of 'the sinful among them' is incompatible. By examining the context as a whole, we see that the notion suggested by the particle of exemption ('except') is more appropriate to it than that suggested by the particle of generality ('all'); there is, indeed, no common measure between them. The particle of exemption thus comes to be the element that determines the meaning of the whole context.

The attached contextual element is therefore any word that, connecting to another word, nullifies its apparent meaning and directs the overall meaning of the context in a direction compatible with its own meaning.

Sometimes a contextual element is not directly attached to a given statement, but occurs separately from it, in which case it is termed a detached contextual element (*qarinah munfasilah*).

An example of this possibility would be for someone to give the instruction, 'be generous to all of the poor', and after a while to add, in a separate statement, 'do not be generous to the sinful among the poor'. If the prohibition contained in the second statement had come within the first statement, it would have been considered an attached contextual element, but being included in a separate statement it counts as a detached contextual element.

We can now understand the principle of jurisprudence that 'the apparent meaning of the contextual element has priority over the contextualized word, irrespective of whether the contextual element is attached or detached.'

LESSON FIFTEEN

Verification of Issuance

Before we can consider a statement to constitute legal evidence, we must establish that it indeed issued from one of the Possessors of Infallibility (the Prophet (SAWA) and the Imāms). This can be accomplished in the following ways:

1. *Tawātur*: abundant transmission of the report containing the statement. Such transmission is undertaken by a large number of narrators each of whom constitutes a source of probability for the veracity of the report, an indication of its validity. The accumulation of probabilities and indications leads to certainty that the report in question did indeed emanate from one of the Possessors of Infallibility. *Tawātur* possesses authority because it conveys certain knowledge and is not dependent on anything else.

2. *Ijmā'* and *shuhrah*: consensus and the widely known. To illustrate these concepts, let us take the case of a ruling (*fatwā*) by a jurist regarding the levying of *khums* on minerals. Such a ruling forms what might be termed a partial contextual element pointing to the existence of some verbal evidence before he delivered his ruling. The ruling of a jurist brings two possibilities to mind: he may have relied in a proper fashion on some verbal evidence and based his ruling upon it or he may have delivered an erroneous ruling.

   As long as both these possibilities exist, they are nothing more than a partial contextual element pointing to the existence of verbal evidence. But if we add to the ruling by this jurist a similar ruling by another jurist declaring the payment of *khums* on minerals to be obligatory, the probability of the existence of verbal evidence as a source for the rulings would increase. This increase in probability results from the confluence of the two partial contextual elements. If a third jurist corroborates their ruling, we will be still further inclined to believe in the existence of some verbal evidence specifying that *khums* should be paid on minerals. The inclination to believe in the existence of verbal evidence increases in proportion to the number of jurists giving the same ruling. If all jurists agree on a given ruling, it is termed *ijmāʿ* ('consensus'), and if a majority of them do so, it is called *shuhrah* ('the widely known'). *Ijmāʿ* and *shuhrah* are thus two ways in which the existence of a verbal evidence may sometimes be discovered.

According to legal theory, *ijmāʿ* and *shuhrah* must be taken into consideration in the process of derivation only if they yield knowledge of a verbal evidence, failing which they have no authority. For then they would be based on nothing more than supposition, and revelation contains nothing to substantiate the authority of this or any other kind of supposition.

3. *Sīrat al-mutasharriʿah*: the normative practice of observant believers. By this is meant the general conduct of observant believers living at the time of one of the Posssessors of Infallibility, examples being their agreement on performing the noon prayer instead of the Friday prayer on Fridays and not paying *khums* on inheritance.

If we analysed each individual instance of this general conduct and examined separately the conduct of each person involved, we would conclude that the conduct of each observant believer during the era of legislation may be regarded as a partial contextual element pointing to the existence of some relevant instruction. At the same time, we must bear in mind the possibility of error, ignorance or carelessness lying at the origin of the conduct in question.

If we know that two observant individuals consistently engaged in a certain practice, such as performing the noon prayer on Friday instead of the Friday prayer, this strengthens the likelihood that pertinent verbal evidence exists, a likelihood that increases in proportion to the number of religious people adhering to the same practice. If we then find that the practice in question was followed by a majority of observant believers living in the era of legislation, we conclude that the practice cannot have been the result of error, ignorance or carelessness. Such might be the case if it were a question of only one or two persons, but not with the great mass of observant believers living in the era of legislation.

General conduct of this type thus comes close to being an authoritative declaration, indicating in this particular case the permissibility of saying the noon prayers on Friday and the exemption of inheritors from payment of the *khums*. In most cases, the existence of a legally binding declaration can be categorically inferred from the general practice of observant believers, subject to certain conditions that cannot be elaborated here, which permits us to regard that practice as authoritative. If no such inference can be drawn, the practice has no authority, because there is nothing to indicate that it does.

The three methods reviewed so far are based on the accumulation of probabilities and contextual elements.

4. *Khabar al-wāḥid al-thiqah* (a report narrated by a single trustworthy person only). A report narrated by one person only does not independently establish definite knowledge, and it can be treated as authoritative only if the narrator is trustworthy. The authority of such a report is based not on rational, but on revealed considerations, for it derives not from any ability to provide certainty but from the instruction of the Lawgiver to accept and follow a report narrated by a trustworthy person. Among the numerous pertinent texts is the following verse, known as *Āyat al-Naba'* ('The Verse of the Report'): 'O you who believe, if there comes to you an untrustworthy person with a report, verify its truth' (49/6). The verse consists of a conditional statement, with both explicit and implicit signification.

The explicit is that verification is necessary whenever an untrustworthy person provides a report, and the implicit that such verification is unnecessary when it is a trustworthy person providing the report. The verse therefore establishes the authority of a report narrated only by a single observant and trustworthy person. The normative practice of observant believers and of rational beings in general provides further justification for relying on the solitary report. We deduce this from the fact that observant believers did so, as did the Companions of the Imāms and those who narrated their traditions. This must in turn imply that the authoritativeness of the solitary report is accepted by the Legislator, in accordance with the reasoning that underlies the concept of the normative practice of observant believers.

LESSON SIXTEEN

Non-verbal Religious Evidence

Non-verbal religious evidence includes whatever emanates from a Possessor of Infallibility and is significant for a religious ruling, but does not belong to the category of speech. Such evidence includes the actions of the Possessor of Infallibility, since his performance of an action indicates its permissibility and his omission of it signifies that it is not obligatory. His performance of an action as an act of worship indicates that it is desirable. That the Possessor of Infallibility indeed engaged in these acts is established in the same way that we establish the issuance from him of verbal religious evidence.

Non-verbal evidence also includes a tacit endorsement (*taqrīr*) made by the Possessor of Infallibility. By this is meant that he remains silent regarding an action that takes place in his presence, indicating his tacit approval of the conduct, for if he had disapproved of it, he would necessarily have prevented it. Non-prevention is therefore indicative of approval and acceptability.

'Normative Rational Practice' and the 'Practice of Observant Believers'

Conduct may sometimes be individual in nature and relate to a specific incident. An example would be someone who, making his ablutions in the presence of the Imām , wipes his head out of the prescribed order; in such a case the Imām chooses to remain silent. At other times, a form of conduct may be generic in nature, common to all rational beings; it is then termed 'normative rational practice' (*al-sīrat al-'uqalā'iyya*), which consists of a general tendency among rational beings to behave in a certain fashion without revelation's playing any effective role in the formation of that tendency. Examples of such a tendency are acceptance of the apparent meaning of a statement, acceptance of a report transmitted by a trustworthy person or regarding possession as a proof of ownership of resources available for public use (*al-mubāḥāt al-awwaliyyah*). Normative rational practice differs from 'the practice of observant believers', this being a means for discovering the issuance of a *shar'i* evidence, for it usually results from a *shar'i* instruction and reflects it in turn, just as an effect points to its cause. 'Normative rational practice', by contrast, results from a general tendency among rational beings to a particular mode of conduct, based not on *shar'i* instructions but on other elements and factors affecting the behaviour of rational people. 'Normative rational practice' is not therefore confined to believers, because revelation has not influenced its formation.

It follows from this argument that 'normative rational practice' does not indicate the existence of a prior *shar'i* instruction, again in conformity with the principle that an effect points to its cause. It may, however, indicate a *shar'i* ruling insofar as it is supported by a tacit endorsement by the Possessor of Infallibility. This can be explained as follows. The tendency of rational beings to a particular mode of conduct also acts as a factor impelling them to its practice. If that tendency is not rejected by the *Sharī'a* and the conduct in which it eventuates is not opposed by the Possessor of Infallibility when practised in his presence, this signifies tacit approval on his part of the tendency in question. An example of this is provided by the silence of the *Sharī'ā* on the common tendency among rational beings to take the apparent meaning of a statement to be its real meaning. This tendency is not rejected by the Possessor of Infallibility, signifying that the *Sharī'ā* approves of this method for the understanding of a statement; for if this were not the case, it would have forbidden conformity with the tendency underlying it.

The authority of apparent meaning can therefore be vindicated with respect to the normative practice of rational beings, in addition to the support provided by the practice of observant believers contemporary with the Messenger and the Imāms (AS).

LESSON SEVENTEEN

Rational Evidence; Rational Relationships

When reason examines the relationships existing among different things, it recognizes that there are different types of relationship. It perceives, for example, a relationship of contradiction existing between black and white, resulting in the impossibility of their concurrence in a single object. It also realizes that there is a relationship of necessity between a cause and its effect, since every effect is a rationally necessary outcome of its cause and cannot be detached from it, an example of this being the relationship of heat with fire. Additionally it perceives a relationship of priority and posteriority to exist between a cause and its effect. An example of this is provided by a hand turning a key in a lock, for although the key turns at the very moment that the hand turns it, reason considers the movement of the hand prior to the turning of the key and the turning of the key as posterior to the movement of the hand. The priority of the hand is not temporal, deriving rather from existential sequentiality. When we describe this event with the statement '*ḥarraktu yadī fa taḥarrak al-miftāḥ*' ('I moved my hand and then the key moved'), the particle *fa* before *taḥarrak* indicates that the motion of the key was subsequent to that of the hand despite their simultaneous occurrence. The subsequentiality is not temporal, relating rather to rationally perceived existential sequentiality. In other words, when reason observes the movement of the hand and that of the key and comprehends that the movement of the latter stems from that of the former, it realizes that the movement of the key is posterior to that of the hand, in the sense that it issued from it. It is this posteriority that is indicated by the *fa* in the example we have given, a posteriority known as 'posteriority in rank.'

Once it comprehends relations such as these, reason can make use of them in order to discover the existence or non-existence of certain things. Through the relationship of contradiction existing between blackness and whiteness, reason can establish the non-existence of blackness in a white object, because of the impossibility of the concurrence of whiteness and blackness in a single object. Through the relationship of necessity existing between a cause and its effect, reason can prove the existence of an effect whenever it knows of the existence of its cause, by virtue of the impossibility of separation between the two. By understanding the relationship of priority and posteriority, reason can establish the impossibility of existence of the posterior before the existence of the prior, for this would contradict its being a posterior. Thus if the motion of the key is rationally posterior to that of the hand in terms of existential sequentiality, it is impossible for the motion of the key to precede that of the hand.

Just as reason comprehends the various relationships existing between different things and has the ability to deduce from them the existence or non-existence of a thing, so too it can comprehend the relationships existing between the laws. Similarly, it has the ability to deduce from these relationships the existence or non-existence of particular laws. For example, it understands a contradiction to exist between obligation and prohibition just as it does in the case of blackness and whiteness. In the same way it employed that relationship to negate the blackness of a white object, it employs the relationship of contradiction between obligation and prohibition to negate the possibility that an act may be obligatory when it is known to be prohibited. So, just as reason examines relationships between things, it also examines relationships between rulings.

We designate the totality of things as 'the world of creation' (*al-ʿālam al-takwīnī*) and the totality of legislative rulings as 'the world of legislation' (*al-ʿālam al-tashrīʿī*).

Just as reason can discover the existence or non-existence of a thing in the world of creation by means of different types of relationship, so too it can also discover the existence or non-existence of rulings in the world of legislation by precisely the same method. It is therefore a necessary part of the discipline of the principles of jurisprudence to study these relationships as they affect rulings, for they are rational propositions fit to be used as common elements in the process of derivation. We will now consider examples of these relationships.

One type of relationship encountered in the world of legislation is that existing among the rulings themselves, i.e. between one *shar'i* ruling and another. A second type of relationship exists between a ruling and its subject matter; a third exists between the ruling and its referent; a fourth exists between a ruling and its prerequisites; a fifth consists of relationships existing within a ruling itself; and the sixth type comprises relationships existing between the ruling and things lying outside the boundaries of the 'world of legislation.'

LESSON EIGHTEEN

Relationships Existing Among Different Rulings: the Relationship of Contradiction Between Obligation and Prohibition

It is acknowledged in the science of *uṣūl* that it is not impossible for a *mukallaf* (person subject to *shar'i* answerability) simultaneously to perform two acts, one of which is obligatory and the other prohibited. He counts as obedient and deserving of reward for performing the obligatory act, and as disobedient and deserving of punishment for committing the prohibited act. An example of this is provided by a person who drinks ritually unclean water while paying *zakāt* at the same time.

One and the same action cannot, however, count as both obligatory and prohibited. The relationship between obligation and prohibition is one of contradiction, and they cannot both occur in a single action, just as blackness and whiteness cannot concur in a single object. Thus paying *zakāt*, which is obligatory, cannot simultaneously be prohibited, nor can the drinking of ritually unclean water, which is prohibited, be simultaneously obligatory.

Two conclusions follow from this:

First, in the case of two distinct acts, such as paying *zakāt* and drinking ritually impure water, it is possible for one of them to be qualified as obligatory and for the other as prohibited, even if both are undertaken simultaneously by the same individual.

Second, one and the same act cannot count as both obligatory and prohibited.

The importance of this discussion for the scholars of *uṣūl* lies in the fact that an act can be described as one with respect to its essence and existence, but as multiple with respect to its attributes and designations. Should then the act be regarded as one because of its existential unity, or as multiple because of its attributes and designations?

An example of this would be making ablution with stolen water. When considered in terms of its essence and existence, this act constitutes a single entity, but it may be described in two different ways when its attributes are taken into consideration. For what is transpiring can be described as the making of ablution, but also as an act of theft, the utilization of another's property without his permission. These different descriptions of the same act are termed 'designations' (*'anāwīn*). The act in question is thus singular in existence and essence but multiple in description and designation.

The scholars of *uṣūl* hold two different opinions on this matter.

The first is that a procedure such as the one described constitutes two different acts by virtue of its multiple descriptions and designations. Thus, just as it is possible to describe the payment of *zakāt* as obligatory and the drinking of ritually unclean water as prohibited, even when both are performed at the same time by the same person, it is possible that one of the descriptions and designations of the procedure we have described be obligatory – making the ablution – and another of them be prohibited – the theft of the water. This opinion is known as *'al-qawl bi jawāz ijtimā' al-amr wa al-nahy'* ('belief in the possibility of concurrence of command and prohibition in a single procedure').

The second opinion holds that such a procedure must be considered a single act because of its existential unity. Multiplicity in description and designation cannot alone justify attributing both obligation and prohibition to a single procedure. This opinion is known as *'al-qawl bi imtinā' ijtimā' al-amr wa al-nahy'* ('belief in the impossibility of concurrence of command and prohibition').

The question is then whether multiplicity of description and designation in a single act can justify the simultaneous occurrence of obligation and prohibition in the procedure of making ablution with stolen water. Or is it rather the case that as long as the procedure is singular in terms of existence and essence it cannot have the attributes of both obligation and prohibition at the same time?

Some argue that, since rulings are conceptual entities that exist in the mind of the one who issues them, they are connected only to mental forms and designations and have no direct relationship to external reality. This multiplicity of designations and mental forms solves the problem and makes possible the simultaneous occurrence of command and prohibition with respect to a single act.

Others, however, argue that although rulings are connected to mental forms and designations, they are not connected to them primarily as such, for it is evident that the lawgiver is concerned with those forms only insofar as they express and reflect external reality. The external reality of an act being singular, it is impossible that both obligation and prohibition should exist in it, even if mediated by two designations or mental forms. It is therefore said that if a multiplicity of designations results from a multiplicity in external reality, thereby expressing its diversity, it is possible for command to be attached to one designation and prohibition to another. Multiplicity of designation and mental form in the mind alone, not in external reality, does not point to this conclusion.

Does Prohibition Necessitate Invalidity?

The validity of a contract means that the consequences that have been agreed upon by the contracting parties should be put into effect. Thus, as regards a contract of sale, it will be considered valid and binding if it results in transference of ownership of the commodity from the seller to the buyer and transference of the money from the buyer to the seller. It is self-evident that one and the same contract cannot be both valid and invalid at the same time, for validity and invalidity contradict each other, just as obligation and prohibiton contradict each other.

The question is, however whether one and the same contract can be both valid and prohibited. The answer is in the affirmative, for no contradiction exists between validity and prohibition, just as there is no necessary connection between prohibition and invalidity. The meaning of the contract's being prohibited is that the legally answerable is forbidden to conclude it, while the meaning of its being valid is that if the person were to disregard the prohibition and sell the commodity in question, the sale would take effect and ownership would be transferred from the seller to the buyer. There is no contradiction between the making of a contract that is deplored and prohibited by the Lawgiver on the one hand, and that contract entering into effect once it has been made on the other hand. An example of this would be the type of divorce known is *ẓihār*, which is forbidden by the *Sharī'ā* but comes into effect once it has been pronounced.

A somewhat comparable situation may occur in everyday life. You may not wish a certain person to visit you, and even strongly resent it if he does. But if he happens to visit you, the formalities of the visit impose themselves on you and you show him hospitality.

A certain transaction, such as a contract for the sale of some commodity, may be prohibited, but this does not invalidate it. This is contrary to the view of a number of scholars who hold that prohibition of a transaction renders it invalid.

Just as prohibition is attached to certain contracts and transactions, it may also be attached to matters of worship such as fasting on the day of 'Id or prayer performed by a menstruating female. However, in contrast to contracts and transactions, prohibition in matters of worship does invalidate the act of worship in question. The reason for this is that matters of worship are not valid unless performed with the intention of drawing closer to God, and once an act of worship has been prohibited, it is impossible to intend to draw closer to God by means of it; He cannot be approached by means of disobedience. Hence the act in question is invalid.

Relationships Existing Between a Ruling and its Subject and Those to Whom it Applies: Stipulation and Actualization

Once the *Sharī'ā* commanded that 'pilgrimage to the House is a duty men owe to Allah, for those who can afford it' (03:97), the *ḥajj* became, by virtue of that commandment, an obligatory practice in Islam. If, however, we were to suppose that at the time in question there did not exist a single individual among the Muslims who had the requisite ability as defined by the *Sharī'ā* to perform the pilgrimage, no one would have been actually subject to that obligation. Hence the obligation of pilgrimage, despite being a firmly established law of the *Sharī'ā*, would not have pertained to a single individual Muslim. As soon as an individual attained the requisite ability, the obligation would become applicable to him and established for him.

We thus see that the ruling on pilgrimage had two modes of establishment: one in the body of the *Sharī'ā* and the other with respect to a given individual. This means that if someone at that time were to have asked for a listing of the ordinances of Islam, the obligation of pilgrimage for those able to afford it would certainly have been included, irrespective of whether or not anyone with the requisite means actually existed. The ruling stipulating the obligatory nature of the *ḥajj* as a part of the *Sharī'ā* thus depends exclusively on its having been established by Allah as the Legislator, irrespective of its actual practice or lack thereof among the Muslims.

By contrast, the obligatory nature of the *ḥajj* with regard to a given individual depends not only on the existence of the divine legislation but also on his possessing the requisite ability to perform it. A ruling is thus established in two ways: by means of 'stipulation' (*ja'l al-ḥukm*), at the level of legislation, and by means of actualization (*fi'liyat al-ḥukm*), whenever adherence to a ruling becomes incumbent on a given individual.

The Subject of the Ruling

The 'subject of the ruling' (*mawḍu' al-ḥukm*) is a term used in *uṣūl* to denote the totality of things upon which the actualization of the ruling depends. In the case of the pilgrimage, the existence of an individual able to perform it is the subject of this obligatory ruling, because its actualization is dependent upon him.

Another example of this is provided by the fast, stipulated by the *Sharī'ā* as obligatory for every legally responsible person who is neither travelling nor sick when the crescent moon marking the beginning of Ramadan becomes visible to him. The first establishment of this ruling depends only on its being legislatively stipulated, but its second establishment – i.e. realization – depends on the existence of its subject, a legally responsible person as described above. The existence of a such a person, together with the fact that he is neither travelling nor sick at the time the crescent moon becomes visible, are the elements that together form the complete subject for the ruling on the obligatory nature of fasting. The relationship between the ruling and its subject is similar in some respects to that existing between the effect and its cause, as for example as heat and fire. For as the effect is dependent upon its cause, the ruling is dependent on its subject, since it is from the existence of the subject that it gains its actuality. It is therefore said that 'the actualization of a ruling depends on the actualization of its subject'; i.e. the actual existence of the ruling is dependent on the actual existence of its subject. Because of this relationship between the ruling and its subject, a ruling is regarded as existentially posterior to its subject just as an effect is posterior to its cause.

A number of matters result from this relationship of posteriority that are relevant to *uṣūl* and may be applied in the process of derivation. One is the impossibility that the subject of the ruling be an effect of the ruling itself. An example of this is 'knowledge of the ruling', which is naturally caused by the ruling itself, insofar as the knowledge of a thing is secondary to its existence. It follows that it is impossible to consider the knowledge of a ruling to be the subject of the ruling itself. Hence the Lawgiver cannot say, 'I rule that this ruling be obeyed by whoever knows of this ruling,' since this would lead to a circular argument.

Relationships Existing Between the Ruling and its Referent

We have seen in the case of the obligation of fasting that its subject is composed of several factors upon which the actualization of the obligation depends. As for the referent (*muta'alliq*) of this obligation, it is the act performed by the legally responsible person once the obligation has been directed to him, which in this case is fasting. There is, therefore, a difference between the referent and the subject of the obligation. Whereas the referent exists by virtue of the obligation, so that the fasting of the *mukallaf* is due to the obligation of fasting, the ruling itself exists by virtue of the existence of the subject, while also being a cause for the emergence of the referent and a factor impelling the *mukallaf* to act. It is therefore impossible for the obligatoriness of a ruling to bring its subject into being and summon the *mukallaf* to action, by contrast with its referent. Thus the obligatoriness of fasting for every *mukallaf* who is neither travelling nor sick cannot compel a given individual not to travel but only to fast if he is not travelling. Likewise, the obligatoriness of pilgrimage for those who have the means cannot compel a given individual to work in order to acquire the means; it simply ordains it for those who do have the means.

The reason for this is that a ruling exists only after the existence of its subject, prior to which no ruling can exist calling for the creation of its subject: hence the principle in *uṣūl* to the effect that 'it is impossible for any ruling to impel a person towards any of the elements that form its subject, the effects of the ruling being restricted to the scope of its referent'.

The Relationships Existing Between a Ruling and its Preliminaries

The preliminaries (*muqaddimāt*) upon which the existence of an obligatory act depends are twofold:

1. those on which the existence of the referent is dependent, such as travelling in the case of the *ḥajj*, ablution in the case of prayers or arming oneself in the case of *jihād*.

2. those that play a part in the genesis of the subject of obligation, such as the intention of residing in one place on which fasting in the month of Ramadan is contingent, or the possession of means on which making the *ḥajj* is contingent.

Let us examine the difference between the two types. The obligatoriness of the act itself is contingent on preliminaries of the second type, in view of the fact that the existence of religious ruling is dependent upon the existence of its subject. Every preliminary of this type is therefore a precondition for the existence of the ruling itself. As for the preliminaries that have no influence on the formation of the subject of the ruling, but on which the existence of its referent depends, the ruling does exist prior to and independently of their existence, for they do not form its subject.

By way of further explanation, let us take the examples of the possession of means for performing the *ḥajj* and the ablution required for prayer. The possession of means is a preliminary upon which the *ḥajj* depends; earning money is in turn a preliminary to the possession of means; and going to one's place of work is a preliminary to earning money. Since the possession of means plays a part in the genesis of the subject of the obligatoriness of the *ḥajj*, the *ḥajj* is not obligatory before the possession of means and everything on which that possession depends.

By contrast, the ablution required for prayer does not play any role in the genesis of the subject of the obligatoriness of prayer, for that obligatoriness does not wait on the performance of ablution by a given individual before it is directed to him. The only thing that is dependent on the ablution is the referent of the obligation, i.e. the prayer itself. As for the ablution, it is dependent on obtaining the water with which it is performed, this in turn being dependent on turning the tap.

We find therefore two chains of preliminaries:

First, one for the referent, an example being the ablution on which depends the performance of prayer, and which depends in turn on obtaining water and that in turn on turning the tap.

Second: one for the obligation, an example being the possession of means, which plays a role in the genesis of the subject of the obligation of pilgrimage, this in turn depending on earning money and that in turn on going to one's place of work.

The attitude of obligation towards this second chain and all the preliminaries included in it is always passive, in the sense that the existence of its subject depends on them and, as we have already seen, an obligation cannot call for its own subject. The preliminaries included in this category are termed 'preliminaries of obligatoriness' (*muqaddimāt al-wujūb* or *muqaddimāt wujūbiyyah*).

But in the case of the first chain and the preliminaries it includes, the *mukallaf* does have the responsibility of fulfilling them, so that a person who has the duty of praying is also responsible for performing the ablution that is its necessary preliminary. Similarly, a person whose duty it is to perform the *ḥajj* has the responsibility to undertake the travel that is its necessary preliminary, and one whose duty it is to wage *jihād* has the responsibility of arming himself.

The nature of the responsibility involved has been debated by the scholars of *uṣūl*. They have offered two explanations. The first is that in the case of the prayer what is obligatory on the *mukallaf* is not only the prayer itself but also its preliminaries, including the ablution and other forms of preparation. However, the obligatory nature of the preliminaries is rationally deduced by the *mukallaf* from his understanding that the obligatory act of prayer could not be fulfilled without those preliminaries.

The second explanation is that those preliminaries are made obligatory by the *Sharī'ā*, because the preliminary to an obligatory act is obligatory according to the *Sharī'ā* itself. In light of this second explanation, the *mukallaf* has then two duties to perform, each made independently obligatory by the *Sharīʿā*: the prayer itself and the ablution that is a preparation for prayer. The first of these two duties is termed 'intrinsically obligatory' (*al-wājib al-nafsi*), for it is obligatory in its own right and for its own sake, while the second is termed 'extrinsically obligatory' (*al-wājib al-ghayri*), because it is obligatory for the sake of other than itself, i.e. that to which the ablution serves as preliminary, the prayer.

The second explanation is that offered by those scholars who believe in the existence of a necessary relationship between the obligatoriness of an act and the obligatoriness of its preliminary, so that whenever the Lawgiver ordains an act as obligatory He simultaneously ordains its preliminaries as obligatory.

To this it may be objected that the Lawgiver's making an obligation out of the preliminary obligatory serves no purpose and corresponds to no need. If the intention is to have the *mukallaf* fulfil the preliminary, this purpose has already been attained, for the intellect realizes the necessity of fulfilling the preliminary on which an obligatory act depends. And if the Lawgiver had some other purpose in making the preliminary obligatory, this would lie beyond our comprehension. Making the preliminary obligatory would in either case be purposeless, and could not therefore occur, let alone be necessary.

LESSON TWENTY-ONE

The Relationships Existing Within a Single Ruling

Obligatoriness sometimes pertains to a single act, such as prostration which is obligatory for anyone who hears the recitation of a Qur'ānic verse containing a mention of prostration. At other times, however, its referent may be a process composed of different parts and consisting of several actions, such as the obligation of performing prayer, a process made up of elements such as verbal recitation, prostration, bowing, standing and sitting.

In such cases, the entire process becomes obligatory as the compound of those elements, and each element is also obligatory in its own right. The term used to describe an obligation composed of several parts is, with respect to the whole, 'independent obligatoriness' (*al-wujūb al-istiqlālī*), while the term 'implicit obligatoriness' (*al-wujūb al-ḍimnī*) is used for the obligatoriness of each of its components: 'implicit', because the obligatoriness pertains to the component insofar as it is a part of the whole and not independently, in isolation from the other components.

It is for this reason that the obligatoriness of every part of the prayer is connected with that of the other parts, for the instances of implicit obligatoriness found in each part of the prayer merge with each other to form a single independent obligatoriness. A relationship of concomitancy thus comes into being among those instances, by which is meant that none of them may be separated or detached from another, and if one is voided the others too will be voided.

Let us take the obligation of ablution as an example. It is composed of several parts such as washing the face, washing the right hand and arm, washing the left hand and arm and wiping the head and the feet. Each of these parts is characterized by implicit obligatoriness insofar as they are parts of the obligatory ablution. If, however, an individual is unable to wash his face because of an ailment with the result that the obligation related to that part of the ablution is voided, the obligation related to other parts will also inevitably be voided. The individual in question will not have to discharge the obligation of washing his hands for as long as he is unable to wash his face, for all the separate instances of implicit obligatoriness derive from and relate to the entire process of making ablution. The independent obligatoriness of the process that is made up of those instances is either voided as a whole or affirmed as a whole, and it is not subject to partition or division.

Now, as ablution is characterized by independent obligatoriness, so too is the supplication (*du'ā*) contained in the prayer. There is a difference between a case in which the ablution cannot be performed at all and a case in which ablution might be possible were it not for an impediment, for example, an inability to wash the face. In the first case, the impossibity of ablution leads only to the voiding of its own obligatoriness; that of the supplication remains. In the second case, however, when it becomes impossible to wash the face and its implicit obligatoriness is voided, the obligatoriness of the whole act of ablution will be voided, together with all its implicitly obligatory components.

It may be objected that an individual commanded to perform the prayer who becomes mute and unable to make the necessary oral recitations is still required to perform the prayer, minus the recitations. This could be taken as indicative of the permissibility of separating instances of implicit obligatoriness from each other and as contradicting the existence of concomitancy among them.

The answer to this objection is that the continued obligatoriness of prayer for such a person does not amount to subdividing the obligatoriness of a complete prayer. It is a separate obligatoriness in its own right, addressing itself from the outset to silent prayer. The obligatoriness of a complete prayer and the command conveying it have been voided as a result of the impossibility of making oral recitation; they have been replaced by a new obligatoriness and a new command.

The Primacy of Rational Caution

In the foregoing, we presented the common elements involved in the process of derivation that are embodied in the securing evidences (*al-adillah al-muḥrizah*). We examined their various types and characteristics and distinguished those that have authority from those that do not.

We wish now to study the common elements that are employed in a different type of derivation, that in which the jurisconsult is unable to obtain any evidence indicating a *shar'i* ruling, with the result that the ruling remains unknown to him. His task is then to try to determine the practical stance to be adopted with regard to the unknown ruling instead of uncovering the ruling itself.

An example of this is provided by the issue of smoking. Let us take as our point of departure the probability that it is forbidden by the Sharīʿā. We first endeavour to find evidence for a *shar'i* ruling on the issue of smoking, and when we are unable to do so, we ask ourselves about the practical stance to be adopted towards the unknown – and unknowable – ruling. Is it incumbent on us to observe caution (*iḥtiyāṭ*) in the matter? This is the basic question the jurist now has to answer, and he attempts to do so by having recourse to the practical procedures (*al-uṣūl al-ʿamaliyya*) that count as common elements in the process of derivation. It is these procedures that we shall now study.

When we confront an issue for which the *shar'i* ruling is unknown, is it incumbent on us to observe caution? In order to understand the primary procedural principle that will permit us to answer this question, it is necessary to go back to the source that imposes on us the duty of obedience to the Lawgiver. We must then see whether it imposes upon us recourse to caution in cases of doubt where there is no evidence pointing to either permissibility or impermissibility. Let us therefore define that source – reason. Reason causes us to understand that God has a claim of obedience on His servants, and it is by obeying Him that the claim is fulfilled.

We therefore proffer our obedience to God and adhere to *shar'i* rulings because reason instructs us to do so, not because the Lawgiver has so commanded us. Were we to do so in pure obedience to the Lawgiver, the question would still remain: why should we obey God by executing His commands, and what is the source imposing that obedience upon us? The questioning would continue until we reached the conclusion that reason decrees obedience to be obligatory based on God's claim to obedience.

We must also refer to reason in our attempt to answer the question posed above and establish the boundaries – if any – of God's claim of obedience on us. Is this claim confined to the rulings that are known to us, so that obedience is not due to him in matters not regulated by rulings known to us? Or does the claim of the Lawgiver to our obedience also include cases for which a ruling may probably exist? If the latter be the case, we must not only fulfil those duties that are known to us but also exercise caution with respect to commandments that are probable. This we do by refraining from whatever is probably forbidden and fulfilling whatever is probably obligatory.

The correct view in our opinion is indeed that the primary principle regarding every probable ordinance is caution because such ordinances are encompassed by God's claim of obedience. For reason comprehends that the Lord has a claim of obedience in relation to probable as well as known commands, as long as there is no evidence suggesting that He does not require caution of us in such matters.

The primary principle to be observed in matters of probable prohibition or obligation is therefore caution, avoiding what we suspect to be unlawful and accomplishing what we think obligatory. This principle may be ignored only if there is evidence that the Lawgiver does not consider the probable obligation important enough to warrant our exercise of caution, in which case the *mukallaf* is freed of all responsibility in the matter.

The exercise of caution is rationally obligatory in cases of doubt. Its obligatoriness is termed 'the primacy of caution' (*aṣālat al-iḥtiyāṭ*) or 'the primacy of concern' (*aṣālat al-ishtighāl*), since it is the responsibility of an individual to concern himself with probable commands. We are acquitted of this responsibility only when we know the Lawgiver to be content with our abandonment of caution in such cases.

A large number of scholars are, however, of a contrary opinion. They believe the basic principle to be that the *mukallaf* is not responsible for the fulfilment of doubtful duties, even if he suspects them to be of great importance. Reason, they hold, rejects any such responsibility and regards as abhorrent the punishing of a *mukallaf* for failing to perform duties that have not been communicated to him. They therefore consider the primary principle to be 'the abhorrence of punishment in the absence of declaration' (*qubḥ al-'iqāb bi lā bayān)* or 'rational exemption' (*al-barā'at al-'aqliyyah*). The second of these designations arises from their belief that it would be rationally abhorrent for the Lord to punish the *mukallaf* for failing to heed commands the existence of which is doubtful. The *mukallaf* thus has no need to fear punishment; he is under no responsibilty with regard to such commands nor does he have any need to exercise caution.

They also cite in support of their view 'the normative conduct of rational beings', which decrees that masters cannot hold their subordinates accountable for failing to perform duties the existence of which is doubtful and unproven.

In order to understand whether reason does indeed regard as abhorrent the accountability of the *mukallaf* in such cases, it is necessary to ascertain the boundaries of God's claim of obedience. If it be established that this claim embraces doubtful commands presumed by the *mukallaf* to be of great importance, his punishment for failing to obey them cannot be regarded as abhorrent, for he will have violated the rights of his Lord. As for the argument based on 'the normative conduct of rational beings,' it does not apply to this case, for it establishes only that the right of obedience in the case of worldly masters is limited to known obligations; there is no reason to assume that God's claim to obedience is similarly limited. No objection can be made to distinguishing the two claims from each other and maintaining that one is greater than the other. The primary procedural principle remains, therefore, 'the primacy of caution'.

LESSON TWENTY-THREE

The Secondary Procedural Principle

This primary procedural principle is sometimes transformed, by order of the Lawgiver, into a secondary procedural principle known as 'the primacy of exemption' (*isālat al-barā'ah*), which annuls the necessity of caution. Such transformation occurs whenever we know, by means of an explicit *shar'i* declaration, that the Lawgiver is not concerned with a probable obligation to the degree that would impose the exercise of caution on the *mukallaf*; He therefore consents to our abandonment of caution.

This is indicated by numerous authoritative *shar'i* texts. One of the most celebrated is the saying of the Prophet (SAWA), 'My community is not held responsible for what it does not know'. Also relevant to the principle is the verse, 'It is not Our wont to chastise until We send a messenger' (*al-Isrā'*, 15). 'Messenger' is understood to imply here the provision by God of clear explanation and evidence, so that the verse signifies the absence of chastisement for an act or an omission concerning which there is no clear evidence. The procedural principle is then changed from the necessity of caution to the absence thereof, and the rational principle of 'the primacy of concern' is replaced by the *shar'i* principle of 'the primacy of exemption.'

This secondary procedural principle embraces equally instances of doubt regarding obligation and prohibition, given that the tradition cited above is absolute in its force. Doubt concerning obligation is termed *al-shubahāt al-wujūbiyya* and doubt concerning prohibition is termed *al-shubahāt al-taḥrīmiyyah*.

The principle covers all cases of doubt, whatever be the cause. We therefore adhere to it whether the doubt arises from uncertainty concerning the establishment of a ruling by the Lawgiver or from uncertainty concerning the realization of the subject of the ruling. An example of the first type of doubt is that relating to the obligatory nature of the 'Id prayer or the impermissibility of smoking. Such a doubt is termed 'doubt concerning the ruling' (*al-shubhāt al-ḥukmiyyah*). An example of the second type of doubt is that which arises in connection with the possession of the requisite means for making the *ḥajj*, a doubt that coexists with certainty concerning the obligatory nature of the *ḥajj* for whoever has the means. Doubt of this type is termed 'doubt concerning the subject' (*al-shubhāt al-mawḍū'iyyah*).

More simply, it might be said that in cases of 'doubt concerning the ruling' the *mukallaf* is unsure whether a ruling has been stipulated, and in cases of 'doubt concerning the subject' he is unsure whether the subject of the ruling has been realized. The principle of exemption will apply to both types of doubt.

LESSON TWENTY-FOUR

The Principle of the Accountability (*al-Munajjiziya*) of Summary Knowledge (*al-'Ilm al-ijmāli*)

Consider the following possibilities. You know that your older brother has gone to Mecca; you are not sure that he has gone to Mecca, but you do know that either he or your younger brother has gone to Mecca; and you are unsure whether either of them has gone.

Of these three possibilities, the first illustrates what is termed 'detailed knowledge' (*al-'ilm al-tafṣīlī*), since you know that your elder brother has gone to Mecca, not somebody else, and you have no doubt or confusion in your mind on the matter.

The second illustrates what is termed 'summary knowledge' (*al-'ilm al-ijmālī*), so called because you would then find within yourself two elements fused together – clarity and obscurity. The clarity would be your knowledge that without any doubt one of your brothers has definitely gone to Mecca, and the obscurity would lie in your inability to specify which of the two has gone. Knowledge of this type is termed summary, because it is knowledge insofar as you know one of your brothers to have gone to Mecca, but summary and lacking in detail because you are uncertain which of the two it is that has made the journey.

The possibility that it was the older brother and the possibility that it was the younger are each termed an aspect (*ṭaraf*) of the summary knowledge, because you are sure that one of them has made the journey.

The linguistic form that best conveys summary knowledge of this type, together with its two aspects, is 'either ... or', since in describing the case above you would say, 'either my older brother has gone or my younger brother'. The affirmative dimension of such a formulation represents clarity and knowledge, and the dimension of uncertainty is indicated by 'either ... or.' Whenever the use of a form such as this is possible, it signifies the existence of summary knowledge in our minds.

The third possibility evoked above relates to what is called 'primary doubt' (*al-shakk al-ibtidā'i*), 'initial doubt' (*al-shakk al-badawi*), or 'simple doubt' (*al-shakk al-sādhij*), in that it is pure doubt, unmixed with any form of knowledge. The first two designations are used in order to distinguish this type of doubt from the doubt that exists in each aspect of ambiguous knowledge. That doubt results from knowledge, for although you are unsure whether it is your older or your younger brother who has gone to Mecca you do know that one of them has gone. By contrast, doubt in this third case exists at the outset and is not preceded by any form of knowledge.

All three of the situations we have just reviewed may arise in relation to a *shar'i* ruling. For example, we have detailed knowledge the obligation of the morning prayer, but the obligatoriness of the noon prayer on Friday is doubtful, because of the summary knowledge we have indicating either the Friday prayer or the noon prayer to be obligatory on that day. As for the obligatoriness of the 'Id prayer, it is subject to 'initial doubt' for it is not connected to any summary knowledge. All these examples are instances of 'doubt concerning the ruling' (*al-shubhāt al-ḥukmiyyah*).

Similar examples could be cited in connection with 'doubt concerning the subject' (*al-shubhāt al-mawḍū'iyyah*). Thus we may have detailed knowledge that a drop of blood has fallen into a particular vessel, or summary knowledge that it has fallen into one of two vessels. Equally, we may be uncertain whether any blood has fallen into either of the vessels. It is the situation typified by this third possibility – initial doubt, unmixed with any form of knowledge –that is at issue in our discussion of the secondary procedural principle that sometimes supersedes the primary procedural principle.

We turn now to the doubt resulting from summary knowledge in order to see whether or not the secondary procedural principle applies to it as well.

In the light of the preceding, we can analyse summary knowledge in terms of knowledge and doubt both pertaining to both aspects. Thus at noon on a Friday we know that one of two duties is obligatory for us, either the Friday prayer or the noon prayer, but we are uncertain which of the two is obligatory. The knowledge that one of the two is obligatory, qua knowledge, is governed by the principle of the 'authority of certainty,' so that reason will not permit us to abandon both alternatives, the Friday and the noon prayer. Were we to do so, we would have transgressed our knowledge that one of the two is indeed obligatory, whereas knowledge, whether detailed or summary, is rationally authoritative.

The prevalent view in *uṣūl* concerning summary knowledge maintains that the authoritativeness arising from knowledge not only pertains to both aspects or alternatives, but also cannot be removed from them. Further, it is not possible even for the Lawgiver to permit the abandonment of both alternatives, for this would result in disobedience to Him, any more than it would be possible for Him to remove the aspect of authority from detailed knowledge and permit disobedience to it. As for each aspect of summary knowledge taken individually – the Friday prayer or noon prayer on Friday, in the present case – it counts as a doubtful or unknown duty.

It might seem at first glance that cases such as these are governed by the secondary procedural principle, i.e., exemption negating caution in the case of doubtful duties, since each of the aspects refers to a doubtful duty. The dominant view in uṣūl asserts, however, that the two aspects or alternatives of summary knowledge are not covered by the secondary procedural principle. For were it to be applied to both of them, the result would be a cancellation of responsibility (*barā'at al-dhimmah*) for both the noon and the Friday prayers and make it permissible for neither of them to be performed. This would be contrary to the authority of the certainty characterising our knowledge that one of the alternatives is obligatory, for that authority imposes on us the necessity of performing one of the two. Were the Lawgiver to permit the application of the principle of exemption to both the alternatives involved in summary knowledge, it would be tantamount to Him allowing non-conformity with knowledge, an impossibility as previously stated.

Were the principle of exemption to cover one of the alternatives and not the other, it would not result in permission to abandon them both, but it would still be impossible. For if we asked ourselves which of the two should be given preference, we should find ourselves lacking justification for whatever choice we made, since the principle has exactly the same relationship with both alternatives.

It follows from this that neither alternative or aspect can be governed by the secondary procedural principle. Both of them remain subject to the primary procedural principle which stipulates the necessity of caution whenever the secondary principle is inapplicable.

The initial doubt thus differs from the doubt resulting from summary knowledge in that the former is covered by the secondary principle, i.e. exemption, and the latter is subject to the primary principle, i.e. caution.

We realize therefore that it is rationally obligatory upon us to perform both alternatives that arise in the case of summary knowledge. In the example we have used, this means that it is obligatory at noon on Fridays to perform both the noon and the Friday prayers, since they are both subject to the principle of caution.

Such a procedure is known in *uṣūl* as 'definite conformity' (*al-muwāfaqāt al-qaṭʿiyyah*) because by performing both the alternatives the *mukallaf* can be sure that he has conformed with the instructions of his Lord. If on the other hand he abandons both of them, he is guilty of 'definite non-conformity' (*al-mukhālafāt al-qaṭʿiyyah*). The terms 'probable conformity' (*al-muwāfaqāt al-iḥtimāliyya*), and 'probable non-conformity' (*al-mukhālafāt al-iḥtimāliyya*) may both be used to describe the case in which only one of the alternatives is performed and the other is discarded, because there is an equal probability that the *mukallaf* has or has not discharged the duties imposed on him by his Lord.

LESSON TWENTY-FIVE

Dissolving the Ambiguous Knowledge

Suppose you have two glasses of water, both of which or only one of which may be unclean; all that you are certain of is that both of them together are not clean. You would then have the summary knowledge that at least one of them is unclean, although you do not know which. Suppose further that you then discover an impurity in one of the glasses and realize that glass to be contaminated. Your summary knowledge will then dissolve as a result of your acquisition of this detailed knowledge. Once you know one of the glasses to be definitely unclean, you no longer have summary knowledge with respect to it. As for the other, you remain in doubt.

As a result, you can no longer use the linguistic form 'either ... or' used to denote cases of ambiguous knowledge. You can no longer say, 'either this glass or that one is unclean', because you know this one to be definitely unclean, and you have no knowledge of the uncleanness of the other.

The above situation exemplifies what is described in the terminology of *uṣūl* as the 'dissolving of the ambiguous knowledge in detailed knowledge of one aspect and the emergence of initial doubt in relation to the other'. The uncleanness of one of the glasses is now known in detail, while that of the other has become a form of initial doubt after the cessation of the summary knowledge. The detailed knowledge acquires the force of authority, while the initial doubt is covered by the principle of exemption.

Initial doubt, then, is governed by the secondary procedural principle of exemption, but if connected to summary knowledge, it is covered by the primary procedural principle of precaution.

Sometimes, however, it is not fully clear whether the doubt is an initial one or is connected with summary knowledge. An instance of this is what the scholars of *uṣūl* call 'hesitation between the minimum and the maximum'. This hesitation occurs when obligation is attributed to a compound action composed of different parts, such as prayer. We know that this action definitely includes nine specific parts, but are uncertain about the inclusion of a tenth part, given the absence of evidence either proving or disproving it.

In such a case, the jurist attempts to establish the practical stance to be adopted. He asks whether it is necessary for the *mukallaf* to observe caution; after performing the nine parts of the prayer of which he is certain, need he perform the tenth part,which is only probable, in order to be absolutely sure that he has fulfilled his obligation? Or will it be enough for him to perform the nine parts that he knows to be obligatory?

The jurists offer two different answers, each representing a different approach to the case.

The first approach affirms the need to observe caution in conformity with the primary procedural principle, because the doubt relating to the tenth part of the prayer is connected to a form of summary knowledge. That knowledge is the awareness of the *mukallaf* that the Lawgiver has made obligatory on him a certain compound action, but he is uncertain whether it consists of nine or ten parts. The second approach regards the doubt concerning the obligation of the tenth part as covered by the secondary procedural principle, insofar as it is an initial doubt unconnected with summary knowledge. For, according to this second approach, the summary knowledge presumed to exist by the adherents of the first approach is dissolved in a detailed knowledge, i.e. the knowledge of the *mukallaf* that nine parts are obligatory in any case, irrespective of the status of the tenth part.

The detailed knowledge thus leads to the dissolving of the summary knowledge. We cannot therefore use the linguistic form that is used to describe cases of summary knowledge ('either ... or') or state that we know the obligation to consist of either nine or ten parts. What we know is rather that the obligation definitely includes nine parts, and we are uncertain about the tenth. Doubt in relation to the tenth part thus becomes an initial doubt after the dissolving of the summary knowledge, and it is the principle of exemption that will apply.

The correct approach is the second one: the principle of exemption applies to all unknown things whenever there is doubt about their inclusion in an obligation.

LESSON TWENTY-SIX

The Presumption of Continuity (*al-istiṣḥāb*)

The principle of exemption applies, then, in cases of initial doubt (*al-shubhāt al-badawiyyah*), not in cases of doubts connected with summary knowledge.

Another principle in *Sharī'ā*, somewhat similar to the principle of exemption, is that known to the jurists as 'the presumption of continuity' (*al-istiṣḥāb*). What is meant by this is the fixing by the Lawgiver on the *mukallaf* of the obligation to continue to adhere to that of which he was formerly certain but now entertains doubts.

For example, we are certain that water is inherently pure by its nature, but uncertain whether it retains its purity on coming into contact with an agent of impurity. The presumption of continuity dictates that the *mukallaf* should act in conformity with his former state of certainty, which means treating the water as pure in this example.

Adherence to a former state of certainty is, then, a practical matter. If it relates to a question of purity, we act on the basis that the object in question is still pure. If it relates to an obligation, we act on the assumption that the obligation still applies.

The evidence in support of *istiṣḥāb* is this statement of al-Ṣādiq – upon whom be peace – reported by Ḍurārah : 'certainty is not invalidated by doubt'.

We conclude that *istiṣḥāb* applies to every case of an initial doubt where the doubt has been preceded by certainty. The existence of a former state of certainty is, then, a basic condition for the application of *istiṣḥāb*.

That state may at times relate to a general ruling which we know to have been stipulated by the Lawgiver and to exist in the sphere of legislation; however, we do not know the precise coordinates of the ruling nor the extent of its duration in the world of legislation (i.e. whether or not it remains binding). In this case, our doubt relates to the ruling itself and *istiṣḥāb* will accordingly be applied to the ruling, being termed 'presumption of continuation of the ruling' (*al-istiṣḥāb al-ḥukmī*); it will be analogous to the presumption of the continued purity of water after it has come into contact with an agent of impurity. At other times, the state of previous certainty may relate to the 'world of creation' (*al-'ālam al-takwīnī*): we know that something used to exist as the subject of a *shar'i* ruling, but are uncertain whether it still exists. In this case our doubt concerns the subject, and it is to the subject that *istiṣḥāb* is applied.

Example are provided by the presumed continuity of probity on the part of a leader who is suspected of becoming corrupt and the presumed continuity of the impurity of a garment where there is doubt that it has been cleansed. Such cases exemplify what is termed 'presumption of continuation of the subject' (*al-istiṣḥāb al-mawḍū'ī*), since what is presumed is the continuing existence of the subject of the *shar'i* ruling: the permissibility of praying behind the leader in the first example and the impermissibility of wearing the defiled garment to prayer in the second. One school of thought, however, rejects the application of *istiṣḥāb* to doubts pertaining to rulings and restricts it to doubts pertaining to the subject of rulings.

The tradition narrated by Ḍurārah authorizing *istiṣḥāb* clearly relates it to doubts concerning the subject of a ruling, because the doubt that prompted it concerned the occurrence of sleep invalidating ablution. This does not forbid, however, a more general application of the principle, because the Imām's statement, 'certainty is not invalidated by doubt', is general in nature. Those who would argue otherwise must demonstrate the existence of a contextual element necessitating a restrictive interpretation.

Doubt in the continuity of the previous state is the other basic condition for the application of *istiṣḥāb*.

The jurists divide doubt in continuity into two types, depending on the nature of the previous state of certainty. That state may be able by its very nature to extend over time, and the doubt concerning its continuity arises from an external element impeding the continuity.

An example of this is the purity of water, since purity by its nature is continuous and may extend indefinitely in time unless prevented by an external element. If we doubt the continued purity of water, this will be because the water has come into contact with an external element, i.e. an agent of impurity. Likewise, a piece of cloth that we know to be unclean will remain such as long as the external element of washing does not occur.

Doubts of this type relating to the continuity of a previous state are known as 'doubt regarding the remover' (*al-shakk fi al-rāfi'*).

At other times, the previous state cannot, by its very nature, extend indefinitely in time, being bound to terminate of itself at a particular time. Here the doubt is unconnected to the occurrence of any external element. An example of this is provided by the extent of the daylight hours one is obliged to fast during the month of Ramadan and doubt occurs whether or not the hours are at end. Those hours necessarily end of their own accord and cannot extend indefinitely in time, so the doubt about their possible continuation cannot be due to any external factor.

Doubts of this type concerning the continuity of previous states are called 'doubt regarding the requisite' (*al-shakk fi al-muqtaḍā*) since the doubt relates to the extent of the expediency of daytime and its ability to continue.

Some tendencies in *uṣūl* deny the applicability of *istiṣḥāb* to such cases and restrict it to 'doubt regarding the remover'. In view of the absolute nature of the Imām 's statement, however, the correct view is that the principle may be generally applied.

The jurists agree that one of the conditions for the application of *istiṣḥāb* is the unity of subject, by which they mean that the doubt should pertain to the same state about which we were previously certain. The principle does not apply to cases where the certain and the doubtful states are different. For example, we may be certain that a quantity of water is impure, and the water then turns into steam, and we are unsure whether or not it too is impure. *Istiṣḥāb* will not apply to this case, because our certainty related to the water and our doubt is to the steam. Steam being different from water, the subjects of our certainty and doubt are not the same.

LESSON TWENTY-SEVEN

Contradiction Between the Evidences

We saw previously that evidences are of two types: securing evidences and procedural principles. We will therefore discuss contradiction between evidences under the following three headings:

1. contradiction between two securing evidences;
2. contradiction between two procedural principles;
3. contradiction between a securing evidence and a procedural principle.

The meaning of contradiction between two securing evidences is that their implications are mutually incompatible. Such contradiction can occur between two *shar'i* utterances made by a Ma'sūm ; between a *shar'i* evidence and a rational evidence; and between two rational evidences.

A number of principles are to be observed when we are confronted with contradiction between two verbal evidences.

1. It is impossible that there be two statements made by a Possessor of Infallibility, one of which discloses a definite ruling at variance with the ruling disclosed by the other. This is because two explicit statements of this kind would be tantamount to the Possessor of Infallibity contradicting himself, which is an impossibility.

2. Sometimes one of two comparable statements made by the Possessor of Infallibility has a definite and explicit sense that is apparently contradicted by the explicit sense of the other. An example of this is provided by the following case. We are told by the Lawgiver, through a pronouncement by one of the Possessors of Infallibility, that it is

permissible for a person fasting to submerge his head in the water, while another instruction reads, 'do not submerge your head in the water while fasting'. The first instruction explicitly signifies the permissibility of submerging the head while fasting, whereas the second instruction contains a negative imperative, suggesting prohibition; prohibition is, after all, the apparent meaning of the negative imperative and that which first comes to mind, although it may also be used metaphorically to convey undesirability. A contradiction thus arises between the sense of permissibility explicitly conveyed by the first text and the apparent suggestion of impermissibility made by the second text.

In such a case, it is imperative to uphold the definite and explicit text, since it leads to the knowledge of a religious ruling, and to interpret the apparent text in conformity with its meaning. Here, the negative imperative will be taken to signify undesirability in order to render it compatible with the permissibility conveyed by the definite and explicit text.

In his derivations the jurist thus follows a general principle: affirming evidence of licitness and permissibility whenever it is contradicted by evidence suggesting obligation or prohibition through use of the imperative or negative imperative forms of the verb. The reason for this is that those forms are not explicit in their signification, whereas most evidence pointing to licitness and permissibility is explicit.

3. The subject of the ruling signified by one of the apparently contradictory statements may be more restricted and specific than the subject of the ruling signified by the other. Let us take these two statements: 'interest is impermissible' and 'dealings involving interest between a father and his son are permissible'. The subject of the impermissibility declared in the first statement is general, for it forbids transactions involving interest with any person whatsoever, whereas the subject of the permissibility contained in the second is specific, in that it specifically permits such transactions between father and son.

In a case of this type, the second statement will be accorded precedence, for it is regarded as a defining contextual element of the first by virtue of having a specific subject. For if the speaker were to connect his second statement to the first and say, 'transactions involving interest are prohibited among all people, except fathers and sons', the specific nature of the exception would invalidate the apparently general force of the original statement. As previously demonstrated, the contextual element always takes precedence over that which it defines, whether or not it is directly joined to it.

This precedence of the specific over the general is termed 'qualification of the general' (*takhṣīṣ al-'āmm*) in cases where the generality is established by the particles of generality, and 'restriction of the general' (*taqyīd al-'āmm*) in cases where the generality is established by the absence of any restrictive wording. The specific statement in the first case is called 'the qualifier' (*al-mukhaṣṣiṣ*) and in the second case 'the restrictive' (*al-muqayyid*). In the process of derivation the jurist adheres to the principle of upholding the qualifier and the restrictive and granting them precedence over the general and the unrestricted. The general and the unrestricted remain valid, however, for all cases not excluded by the process of specification and restriction. The reason for this is that evidence cannot permissibly be abandoned beyond the extent to which it is contradicted by stronger evidence.

4. One of two apparently contradictory statements may sometimes imply the existence of a ruling for a subject, while the other statement negates that ruling with respect to certain states by negating the subject. An example would be to say in one statement that '*ḥajj* is obligatory for one possessing the requisite means' and in another that 'a debtor does not possess the requisite means'. The first statement makes the *ḥajj* obligatory for a specific subject, a person possessing the requisite means, while the second negates the possession of requisite means by a debtor. In a case such as this, the second statement will be upheld and is known as 'the overruling' (*al-ḥākim*), and the first is called 'the overruled' (*al-maḥkūm*).

   The principles that necessitate giving precedence to one statement over the other in this and the preceding two cases are known as the principles of 'conventional conciliation' (*al-jam' al-'urfi*).

5. Two apparently contradictory texts may both lack definite and explicit meaning; neither contains any element permitting it to function as a defining contextual element for the other; and neither serves to qualify, restrict or overrule the other. In such a case it is not allowed to act in accordance with either of them, for both exist on the same level and neither is to be preferred to the other.

Cases of contradiction between verbal evidence and other categories of evidence or between two non-verbal evidences are similarly subject to certain general principles, as follows:

1. Definite verbal evidence cannot be contradicted by definite rational evidence, because if rational evidence were at variance with an explicit statement by a Possessor of Infallibility, this would amount to the imputation to him of falsehood and error, an impossibility.

   It is for this reason that scholars of the *Sharī'ā* affirm the impossibility of contradiction between explicit *shar'i* texts and definite rational evidences. This truth is not simply a matter of belief, for it can be confirmed by an examination of the texts of the *Sharī'ā* and a study of the indisputable meaning of the Book and the Sunnah. Everything found there accords with reason, and absolutely nothing contradicts its categorical rulings.

2. A contradiction may exist between verbal evidence and evidence that is neither verbal nor definite. In such a case, precedence is granted to the verbal evidence because it constitutes a proof. Non-verbal evidence does not constitute a proof unless it is characterized by certainty.

3. A contradiction may exist between non-explicit verbal evidence and definite rational evidence. In such a case the latter will be given preference over the former, because the rational evidence leads to knowledge of a religious ruling, while the non-explicit verbal evidence has signification only at the level of apparent meaning. Signification at that level is authoritative, according to the Lawgiver, as long as its falsity is not known. If, however, the apparent meaning of non-explicit verbal evidence conflicts with definite rational evidence, we may conclude that the Possessor of Infallibility did not intend the apparent meaning. There is therefore no reason to act in accordance with it.

4. Two non-verbal evidences may contradict each other. In such a case, it is logically impossible that both of them should be definite; only one can be, and it is that that we should choose.

LESSON TWENTY-EIGHT

Contradiction Between Procedural Principles

The type of contradiction between procedural principles most frequently encountered is that between the principles of exemption (*barā'ah*) and principles of continuity (*istiṣḥāb*). An example is provided by the following case. We know that we are obliged to fast during the daylight hours of the month of Ramadan, from dawn until sunset. We are, however, unsure whether the obligation continues even after sunset, until all redness has disappeared from the horizon. This case includes all the components required by the principle of continuity: certainty about the obligation in the first place and uncertainty about its continuation in the second. Application of the principle of continuity would make it necessary for us to regard the obligation as continuing. However, we find that the same problem falls within the scope of the principle of exemption, because it includes an initial doubt regarding a ruling that is not connected to summary knowledge. Application of this principle to the problem would negate the necessity of observing caution and, in practical terms, free us of the obligation to continue fasting. The question is, then, which one of the two principles should be applied.

All jurists agree that we should uphold and give precedence to the principle of continuity, for they argue that the evidence authorizing the principle of continuity takes precedence over that authorizing exemption. The evidence for the principle of exemption is the statement of the Prophet (SAWA) that frees the believers of obligation in respect to what is unknown to them, and the subject of that evidence is therefore everything that is not known. The evidence for the principle of continuity is the statement that certainty can never be revoked by doubt. If we carefully examine both statements, we realize that the evidence for the principle of continuity eliminates doubt as a factor to be taken into consideration; further, it assumes the state of certainty to be continuing and thereby does away with the subject of the principle of exemption.

In the case mentioned above, it is not therefore possible to have recourse to the principle of exemption, thereby negating the obligation of continuing to fast after the setting of the sun until all redness has vanished from the sky. Such a procedure would involve considering the obligation to be doubtful, whereas the principle of continuity, which enjoys precedence, presumes it to be known.

We come finally to the case of a contradiction between a securing evidence and a procedural principle such as exemption or continuity. In reality, if evidence is definite, contradiction between it and a procedural principle is rationally inconceivable. Definite evidence of an obligation leads to the knowledge of a *shar'i* ruling, and once that knowledge exists, there is no occasion for recourse to any of the procedural principles. Those principles apply only to cases of doubt, the subject of the principle of exemption being whatever is unknown, and that of the principle of continuity being doubt regarding the continuity of that of which we were certain. Whenever the evidence available is definite, the subject of the procedural principles does not exist.

Contradiction between a securing evidence and a procedural principle can arise only when the securing evidence is not definite. Such would be the case if an isolated report narrated by a trustworthy person (which as we have seen is deemed imperative in its force by the Lawgiver, despite its suppositional nature) implied obligation or prohibition while application of the principle of exemption yielded licitness or permissibility.

An example would be a report of that type indicating the impermissibility of a person's immersing his head in water while observing the fast. If we view this impermissibility as based on the report, it counts as a *shar'i* ruling yielded by speculative evidence. If, however, we consider it an unknown obligation, it will be covered by the principle of exemption. In such a case, does the jurist define his stance in accordance with the credible although speculative evidence or does he base himself on the procedural principle?

In such instances, the jurists term the speculative evidence a 'sign' (*amāra*) and describe the contradiction at issue as one between a 'sign' and a procedural principle. They are in no doubt that the isolated report made by a trustworthy person, as well as other types of credible suppositional evidence, has precedence over exemption and other procedural principles. The reason for this is that suppositional evidence has been authorized by the Lawgiver to assume the role of definite evidence. Just as definite evidence negates the subject of the procedural principle and leaves no room for its application, so too does suppositional evidence. Hence it is said that the 'sign' predominates over the procedural principles.

Glossary

adāt al-ghāyah	Particles of extent.
adāt al-sharṭ	The conditional particles.
adāt lughawiyyah	Linguistic forms.
adāt al-'umūm	Particles of generality.
adillah (pl. of *dalīl*)	Proofs, evidences, any proof that could support a religious ruling.
al-adillah al-'amalīyyah	Procedural principles, principles outlining the practical duty in the absence of a religious proof.
al-adillah al-muḥrizah	Securing evidences, those evidences that secure a knowledge of religious rulings.
ahl-al-bayt	(lit. 'household') Technically, the immaculate members of the household of the Prophet (SAWA).
'ālam al-takwīnī	The world of creation.
'ālam al-tashrī'ī	The world of legislation.
amārah	(lit. 'sign') Technically, a jurisprudential evidence.
'āmm	General, unspecified.
al-'anāṣir al-mushtarakah	(lit. 'common elements') Those evidences that are regarded as general principles and could be introduced into different areas of jurisprudence.
al-'anāṣir al-khāṣah	Specific components.
aṣālat al-barā'ah	Principle of exemption.
aṣālat al-iḥtiyāṭ	Principle of precaution.
aṣālat al-ishtighāl	Principle of preoccupation.

aṣālat al-ẓuhūr	Essentiality of the appearance, validity of the manifest meaning of a statement.
aṣl (pl. *uṣūl*)	(lit. 'root') Technically, a source of law or a principle of jurisprudence.
aṣl al-'amali	Procedural principle, principle outlining the practical standpoint in the absence of an evidence.
barā'at al-'aqlīyyah	Rational exemption.
barā'at al-dhimmah	Acquittal of responsibility.
al-dalālah	Indication.
al-dalālah al-taṣdīqiyyah	Sanctional signification, that which discloses the intention of the speaker and requires us not simply to conceive it, but to acknowledge it.
dalīl (pl. *adillah*)	Evidence, proof.
al-dalīl al-ḥākim	The overruling evidence.
al-dalīl al-lafẓī	Textual evidence.
al-dalīl al-maḥkūm	The overruled evidence.
dāll	The indicator.
dhātu mafhūm	Every statement bearing a passive indication, having an implied meaning.
dhi al-qarīnah	Possessor of a consort.
faqīh (pl. *fuqahā'*)	Jurist, religious legal scholar.
fi'līyyatu al-ḥukm	The state of actualization of the ruling.
fiqh	(lit. 'understanding') Technically, the science of jurisprudence.
ḥaqq al- ṭā'ah	The right of obedience.
ḥujjah	Religious proof.
ḥujjiyat al-'ilm	The authority of knowledge.
hujjiyat al-qat'	The authority of certitude.
ḥujjiyyat al-ẓuhūr	The authority of the apparent meaning of a statement.
ḥujjīyyat al-khabar	The validity of a report, authority of reported traditions.
al-ḥukm al-taklīfī	Positive law, defining law, law that defines rights and obligations.
al-ḥukm al-waḍ'ī	Declaratory law, law that regulates and expounds the conditions, exceptions and qualifications of *al-ḥukm al-taklīfī*.
al-ḥukm al-ilzāmī	Binding ruling.
ḥurmah	Prohibition.
ībāḥah	Permission.
īd	prayer Feast prayers, prayers offered on the first day of Shawwal after a month of fast, and

	on the tenth day of Dhu al-Hijjah during the holy pilgrimage to Mecca.
iḥtiyāṭ	Precaution.
ījmā'	Consensus.
ijtihād	The exercise of human reason to ascertain a rule of *Sharī'a*.
al-'ilm al-ijmālī	Ambiguous knowledge.
al-'ilm al-tafṣīlī	Detailed knowledge.
Imāmīyyah	Twelve Shi'ite Muslims.
Iqāmah	Testimonies recited in preparation for obligatory daily prayers.
al-irādah al-isti'mālīyyah	Intention to use a statement in order to signify its linguistic meaning in the mind of the listener.
al-irādah al-jiddīyyah	Serious intention, the intention to induce a meaning in the listener's mind.
istiḥbāb	Desirability.
istiḥsān	Juristic preference, to deem something good.
isti'māl	The usage of a word in its meaning.
istinbāṭ	Inference, deducing a ruling from authorized sources.
istiqrā'	Induction.
istiṣḥāb	Presumption of continuity of a given status.
al-istiṣḥāb al-mawḍū'ī	Presumption of continuation of the subject of the ruling.
al-istiṣḥāb al-ḥukmī	Presumption of continuation of a given ruling.
iṭlāq	Absoluteness, status of being unqualified.
ja'l al-ḥukm	Stipulation of the ruling.
jam'u al-'urfī	Conventional conciliation between too apparently contradictory statements.
jumlat al-sharṭ	The conditional clause.
jumlat al-jazā	The consequence clause.
karāhah	Reprehensibility.
khabar al-thiqah	The report of a trustworthy person.
khabar al-wāḥid al-thiqah	Solitary narration of a trustworthy reporter.
al-khiṭābāt al-shar'īyyah	Revealed discourses.
khums	Religious due on certain properties amounting to one fifth of the original asset.
kurr	A quantity of pure water, which can fill a container of three and a half spans in every dimension (height, length and width) amounting to approximately 378 kg, and which is not affected by ritually impure

	objects as long as none of its colour, smell and taste is changed by it.
liḥāẓ 'ālī	Instrumental observation, what is seen for the sake of something else.
liḥāẓ istiqlālī	Independent observation, what is seen for the sake of itself.
al-ma'nā al-ḥaqīqī	Literal meaning.
al-ma'na al-ḥarfi	Particlar meaning, indicating a type of connection existing among nominal meanings.
ma'ṣūmīn	The infallible.
madkhūl al-adāt	The noun before which a particle has appeared.
madlūl	Any concept or meaning indicated by a statement.
mafhūm al-ghāyah	The implied meaning of the particle of extent.
mafhūm al-sharṭ	The implied meaning of a conditional.
mafḥūm	The implied meaning, the passive indication of a statement.
majāẓ (al-ma'nā al-majāzī)	Metaphorical meaning.
maj'ūl	That which is postulated
manṭūq	The spoken meaning, the positive indication of a statement.
maqām al-bayān	The status of a speaker who intends to explain his intention fully.
muḥrim	One in the state of ritual consecration for the Mecca pilgrimage.
mubāḥāt al-awwalīyah	Primary resources.
mu'adhiriyah	Excusability
mukallaf	Every Muslim who is physically and mentally mature enough to be subject to religious obligations.
mukhālafat al-iḥtimālīyyah	Probable non-conformity.
mukhālafat al-qaṭīyyah	Definite non-conformity.
mukhaṣiṣ	Qualifier.
munajiziīyyah	Accountability.
muqaddamāt	Preliminaries.
muqayyid	Restrictive.
mushtarak	Homonym.
musta'malun fīh	The meaning in which the word is employed.
muṭlaq	Absolute.
muwāfaqāt al-iḥtimālīyyah	Probable conformity.
muwāfaqāt al-qaṭ'iyyah	Definite conformity.

najāsah	Object considered ritually unclean, the state of being ritually unclean.
naṣṣ	Explicit textual ruling.
qāʿidatu qubḥ al-ʿiqāb bi lā bayān	The principle of 'abhorrence of punishment without explanation'.
qarā'in	Contextual evidences.
qarīnah	A consort of the word bearing an indication of the real intention of the speaker.
qarīnah munfaṣilah	Detached consort.
qarīnah muttaṣīlah	Attached consort.
qarīnat al-ḥikmah	Rational consort.
qatʿ	Certitude.
qīyās	Syllogism (logic), analogy (jurisprudence).
ra'y	Opinion.
Ṣādiqain	(lit. 'the two truthful ones') Technically, a word used to signify the fifth and the sixth Shiʿite Imāms together, namely Imām Muḥammad al-Bāqir and Imām Jaʿfar al-Ṣādiq.
ṣaḥīḥ	Valid, authentic.
ṣarīḥ	Unambiguous
al-shakk al-badawī	Initial doubt.
al-shakk al-ibtidā'ī	Primary doubt.
al-shakk al-sādhaj	Simple doubt.
al-shakk fī al-rāfiʿ	Doubt as regards that which may remove the ruling or its subject.
al-shakku fī al-muqtaḍī	Doubt as regards the expedient of the ruling or its subject.
Shāriʿ	The Lawgiver.
Sharīʿa	The divinely revealed sacred law of Islam, the whole body of rules guiding the life of a Muslim.
al-shubha al-ḥukmīyyah	Doubt concerning a ruling.
al-shubha al-mawḍūʿiyyah	Doubt concerning the subject of a ruling.
al-shubha al-taḥrīmiyyah	Doubt with regard to prohibition.
al-shubhāt al-wujūbiyyah	Doubt with regard to obligation.
shuhrah	Repute.
ṣīghat al-amr	The imperative form.
ṣīghat al-naḥy	The prohibitive form.
sīrat al-mutasharriʿah	Normative practice of the committed believers.
sīyāq	Context.
Sunnah	(lit. 'trodden path') Technically, the model conduct and practice of the Prophet (SAWA).

ta'akhur al-rutbī	Being posterior in rank.
tabādur	The spontaneous anticipation of the meaning for which the word is postulated.
ṭahārah	Ritual cleanness.
takhṣīṣ al-'āmm	Qualification of the general in those cases in which generality is established by the particles of generality.
taqrīr	Endorsement, tacit approval.
taqyīd al-'āmm	Restriction of the general in those cases where the generality is established through the unrestricted usage of the word.
tawātur	Continuous recurrence, transmission of a report by a large number of reporters in such a way that rules out any chance of concoction.
thiqah	Trustworthy.
'unwān	Designation.
'urf al-'āmm	Common usage, common practice.
al-uṣūl al-'amaliyyah	cf. *al-adillah al-'amaliyyah*
uṣūl al-fiqh	The discipline of principles of jurisprudence.
uṣūliyyūn	The scholars of *uṣūl al-fiqh*.
waḍ'	Invention, convention, postulation, the procedure of postulating a word for a specific meaning.
al-waḍ' al-ta'ayyunī	Self-specifying postulation, in which a word is postulated for a meaning because of natural or accidental correlation.
al-waḍ' al-ta'īnī	Specifying postulation, in which a postulator stipulates a specific word for a specific meaning.
al-wājib al-ghayrī	Obligatory for the sake of something other than itself.
wājib al-nafsī	Obligatory for itself, on its own accord.
wujūb	Obligation.
al-wujūb al-ḍimnī	Implicit obligation.
al-wujūb al-istiqlālī	Independent obligation.
ẓann	Speculation, conjecture.
al-ẓuhūr al-'urfī	Common manifest meaning.

Transcription System

a	ا	ḍ	ض
b	ب	ṭ	ط
t	ت	ẓ	ظ
th	ث	‘ (*‘ain*)	ع
j	ج	gh	غ
ḥ	ح	f	ف
kh	خ	q	ق
d	د	k	ك
dh	ذ	l	ل
r	ر	m	م
z	ز	n	ن
s	س	h	ه
sh	ش	w	و
ṣ	ص	y	ي
		’ (*hamza*)	ء

Arabic long vowels

ā = آ   ū = و   ī = ي

Persian letters added to the Arabic alphabet

p = پ;   ch = چ zh = ژ   g = گ

Index of Concepts

Index of Names